CREATING SUCCESS!

A program for behaviorally and academically at-risk children

Terri Akin • David Cowan • Gerry Dunne
Susanna Palomares • Dianne Schilling • Sandy Schuster

INNERCHOICE PUBLISHING

ISBN: 0-9625486-42

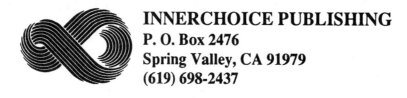

INNERCHOICE PUBLISHING
P. O. Box 2476
Spring Valley, CA 91979
(619) 698-2437

Acknowledgments

The idea for writing *CREATING SUCCESS!* was the result of the collaboration of Innerchoice Publishing and the Lois Craig, Clyde C. Cox, and Gwendolyn Wooley Elementary Schools in the Clark County School District, Las Vegas, Nevada, and more specifically, their principals Noreen Hawley, Al Gourrier, and Teddy Brewer. With their valuable input Innerchoice Publishing has created a comprehensive grade-level approach to prevention education with goals and objectives which are consistent with the body of prevention research and currently accepted prevention program guidelines.

CREATING SUCCESS! has been created to positively influence better behavior and higher academic achievement.

Classroom activities were produced and published by **Innerchoice Publishing**.

Susanna Palomares, Publisher

As human beings we learn best when we:

— *are self-motivated;*
— *feel free to explore personal interests;*
— *take responsibility for our education;*
— *develop a personal relationship with our teacher(s);*
— *feel comfortable in our environment;*
— *get to make important decisions about things that directly affect us;*

Learning and living are essentially the same.

Table of Contents

Preface

The authors are a group of experienced educators who work cooperatively to create innovative programs that reflect proven strategies of teaching and learning.

Education continues to assume more and more responsibility for guiding, nurturing and developing our nation's youth. This fact coupled with concerns regarding individual success and the vulnerability of children to negative influences that lead to high-risk behaviors prompted the development of this activity guide.

We understand the connections between these "at-risk" behaviors and academic risk. We recognize the need to address both.

Activities contained in **CREATING SUCCESS!** are developmentally appropriate and each is identified in its subheading as either K-3 or 4-6. We encourage you to use discretion in selecting activities based on your knowledge of the children with whom you work.

Because we respect the demands on your time, we have given high priority to activities that can be integrated into the core curriculum. We have created activities that expand the focus of teaching because we truly believe that students achieve far more when thinking, feeling, physical sensing, and intuition—all major functions of the brain—are involved in the learning process.

We encourage you to integrate these activities into your classroom in ways that fit your personal style and needs.

The Authors

Introduction

Teachers are like gardeners. A gardener can't "make" a flower bloom. A teacher can't "make" a child learn. A successful gardener places a plant in a nourishing medium, gives it physical support, provides moisture, light, and humidity, monitors the progress of the plant, and adjusts each of the variables to achieve optimum growth. An effective teacher welcomes a child into an intellectually and emotionally enriching environment, offers the child stimulating materials and experiences that engage his/her thoughts, feelings, senses and intuition, listens to and observes the child, and adjusts the materials and mode of instruction to fit the child's progress and preferred style of learning.

The Elements of Risk

Unfortunately, increasing numbers of children come to school not only unprepared to "bloom," but in a condition that has been appropriately termed "at risk." The risk these children face is that, left to influences mostly outside the control of schools, they will do one or more of the following: abuse alcohol and other drugs, become pregnant, act out, drop out, join a gang, and engage in criminal or violent acts.

Many conditions contribute to a child's being "at risk." A 1987 study by Hawkins, Thompson and Gibbs identified several high-risk factors. They include, poverty, teen parenting, residential mobility, single-parent families, violence within the home, involvement with drugs, minimal education, parental substance abuse, criminal conduct or mental illness, and a disfunctional home environment.

Obviously, teachers and other school personnel have little if any direct influence on most of these factors. However, they do have regular, direct contact with the children themselves. And they control a number of variables that have the potential of inducing growth in even the most intellectually and emotionally malnourished student. For some of these children, school may be the only place where positive interpersonal interaction and healthy behaviors are modeled. If school is a welcoming place where children feel they belong, where they regularly receive attention, acceptance, approval, and affection, and where learning experiences are relevant to their needs, there is a chance—perhaps even a good chance—that they will avoid being labeled "at risk," and earn instead the label, "successful."

The Elements of Success

Here are some of the variables over which teachers do have control:

1. **Teachers can create a welcoming environment.** In a nourishing classroom, the climate is one to which children naturally gravitate, one that promotes acceptance, trust, and respect. Rapport is established and maintained between teacher and student and between student and student. Communication is open and frequent positive feedback informs, reinforces, and motivates. This human connection is highly valued.

   Children are given many opportunities to share their feelings. The feeling function of the brain/mind system is recognized and nurtured as a gateway to higher cognitive processes. Children learn positive, healthful ways to express their emotions and are encouraged to accept the emotional experiences of others.

   Children are listened to carefully and often. Listening says "I care" louder than any other behavior. It builds self-esteem. Effective teachers realize that their every word has impact, and so they use empowering language. They focus on what kids do right, not what they do wrong. They communicate high expectations and avoid contributing to self-fulfilling prophecies by labeling children negatively. Empowering language includes questions and responses that challenge children to find their own answers and make their own decisions. Empowering behavior includes listening, showing appreciation, and demonstrating trust in the ability of students to follow through.

2. **Teachers can incorporate relaxation, stress management, and wellness techniques.** The human brain does not function well—indeed learning cannot take place—when a person is in a state of anxiety. Under stress, our retrieval systems are impeded and we forget things. Higher level mental faculties such as intuition and creativity are substantially impaired by fear and stress; therefore, the first step to encouraging higher-level thinking is to *reduce* stress. Consistent reliance on reward-punishment and competitive models in the classroom not only increases stress, but jeopardizes the psychological safety of students. Effective teachers encourage cooperation and self-control. They teach children to pay attention to the physical sensations within their own bodies. They are aware of what can cause tension in the classroom, and take steps to create a stress-free learning environment, even teaching stress management techniques to children.

3. **Teachers can target all learning styles.** Traditionally, education has favored the brain's linguistic and logical/mathematical processes. Children who respond verbally and logically have been rewarded, while those who respond physically or intuitively have been ignored or corrected. Children who are intuitive, artistic, musical, bodily-kinesthetic, interpersonal, and intrapersonal learners have neglected or purposely abandoned these natural inclinations in order to paint themselves in the likeness of the linguistic learner. Effective teachers don't sacrifice talent. They present information so that it can be processed through many learning channels.

4. **Teachers can provide children with choice and perceived control.** Effective teachers ensure that the curriculum remains flexible, with the needs and interests of students providing the base from which activities are developed. They provide simultaneous access to many learning activities, thus encouraging the student to become an active participant in the learning process. Students work in pairs and in small groups. Interaction, cooperation, and teamwork are encouraged.

5. **Teachers can provide challenging cognitive activity.** Effective teachers present learning opportunities corresponding to all levels of Bloom's Taxonomy of Educational Objectives: knowledge and comprehension; application; analysis; synthesis; and evaluation. They utilize a variety of input devices, including reading materials, computer programs, people, videotapes, audiotapes, filmstrips, and experiential activities. Students keep journals, complete research, make maps, build models, invent machines, simulate realities, solve problems and puzzles, develop questionnaires, formulate graphs, diagrams, and charts, create cartoons, commercials, dramas, poems, stories, and songs. They answer thought provoking questions, hold group discussions, make recommendations, and evaluate their own learning.

CREATING SUCCESS!

Components of the Program

CREATING SUCCESS! is a program designed especially for behaviorally and academically at-risk children, grades K-6. It is a collection of experiential activities that provides many challenging and enjoyable ways to infuse the elements of success into the regular curriculum. CREATING SUCCESS! targets eight developmental areas. Children who possess notable attributes and skills in these areas perform better socially as well as academically, and develop high self-esteem.

1. **Expressing Feelings**
2. **Developing Self-Awareness**
3. **Dealing with Stress**
4. **Learning Responsibility**
5. **Problem Solving and Decision Making**
6. **Developing Respect for Self and Others**
7. **Appreciating Differences**
8. **Resolving Conflicts**

Central to the program is a uniquely structured discussion group process called the **sharing circle**. Sharing circles have been extensively tested and shown to provide safe, welcoming environments that promote acceptance, trust, and respect. Sharing circles encourage the expression of feelings and development of listening skills. They ensure that every child has an opportunity to speak and be heard on a regular basis, thus promoting the growth of self-awareness and self-esteem.

CREATING SUCCESS! addresses stress management through activities that incorporate movement, relaxation, and the modeling of healthy lifestyles, and offer skills for resisting peer pressure, a major source of stress in at-risk children. The program utilizes instructional strategies that target many learning styles. Included are activities involving art, music, writing, experiments, drama, and literature, to name a few. Students work in pairs and small groups, as well as individually. Their higher-level thinking skills are challenged through simulations, role plays, problem-solving activities, and in the context of stimulating discussions for which questions are provided at the conclusion of many activities.

Accepting the Challenge

Turning at-risk children into successful students requires enormous commitment and effort. Nurturing the thinking, feeling, physical sensing, and intuitive capabilities of children who enter school already attended by alarming negative forces is neither easy nor does it happen overnight. However, teachers who are committed and willing to do what it takes *will be successful*—and so will their students. The old adage still holds true—anything worthwhile takes work!

Additional Reading:

The authors believe that the following four books are among the most important and valuable resources for educators in print today. Each has a distinct focus but all are aimed at the same goal—making schools more enriching, relevant and exciting places for our nation's youth. We encourage you to read these books; they constitute a solid base of current research and methodology, and will provide a comprehensive theoretical context in which to place the activities in this guide.

1. *Optimizing Learning*

Optimizing Learning
The Integrative Education Model in the Classroom
Barbara Clark, Merrill Publishing Company, Columbus, Ohio
1986

This book provides a thorough grounding in the Integrative Education Model, along with a compelling synthesis of ideas and data from the physicists, psychologists, neurobiologists, and educators whose research forms the model's base. Clark covers the four major functions of the brain—thinking, feeling, physical sensing, and intuition—and explains how they form the structure for a total brain approach to learning and for the development of curriculum. Presented are key components that comprise the organization, conditions, attitudes, and strategies necessary to implement the model in the classroom:
- The Responsive Learning Environment
- Relaxation and Tension Reduction
- Movement and Physical Encoding
- Empowering Language and Behavior
- Choice and Perceived Control
- Complex and Challenging Cognitive Activity
- Intuition and Integration

Optimizing Learning shows how to measure learning by other than graduation requirements and test scores. While integrative education is one way of developing a more brain-compatible curriculum, it also leads to excellence and as Barbara Clark states,
Excellence is more than high ability, more than high levels of performance; excellence allows dreams, visions and idealism and it values love. True excellence is the expression of the uniqueness of each of us; it is the expression of the soul. As teachers, it is our quest to nurture true excellence.

2. *In Their Own Way*

In Their Own Way
Discovering and Encouraging Your Child's Personal Learning Style.
Thomas Armstrong, Ph.D., Jeremy P. Tarcher, Inc.,
Los Angeles, California, 1987

This is a highly readable book that explains some of the reasons so many children do not do well in school. Thomas Armstrong promotes the concept of "learning differences" as an alternative to "learning disabilities." He believes that the reason so many millions of children are underachieving, experiencing school phobias, or just plain bored in the classroom is that no one has recognized and used what they really have to offer—their special talents and abilities. Armstrong's book is based heavily on the work of Howard Gardner of Harvard University, who theorizes that we all have seven different kinds of intelligence—linguistic, logical-mathematical, spatial, musical, bodily-kinesthetic, interpersonal, and intrapersonal. Armstrong teaches us how to perceive children as individuals with distinct intelligences/learning styles and how to help children acquire knowledge according to their sometimes extraordinary aptitudes.

In Their Own Way affirms the rich potential within every child and presents hundreds of ways to help children develop their abilities in and out of the classroom.

3. *Super-Teaching*

Super-Teaching
Master Strategies for Building Student Success
Eric Jensen, Turning Point for Teachers,
Del Mar, California, 1988

In this exciting book, author Eric Jensen challenges teachers to open their eyes to the trends that are affecting education, to focus on the future, to take full responsibility for student learning, and to accept the current challenges in education. He asks that teachers settle for nothing short of the best they can be—and offers over 199 ideas and tools to help begin that journey.

Areas covered in this book are:
- How to open a class with pizazz
- How to teach the "hard-to-teach" student
- How to close a class on a "highnote"
- Five new learning styles and how to identify them
- What the latest brain research means, and what educators should now be doing differently
- Proven ways to boost student interest and motivation
- How to build student self-esteem and self-confidence
- How to boost test scores

4. *21st Century Discipline*

21st Century Discipline
Teaching students responsibility and self-control.
Jane Bluestein, Ph.D., Instructor Books, 1988

This book provides practical and specific strategies to help create a classroom environment in which the majority of student behavior is on track—and the majority of teacher time can actually be devoted to instruction.

Bluestein shows how to develop students who act responsibly in class, come prepared, take care of materials, stay on task, follow rules, and take initiative for their own learning. An excellent guide to non-competitive win-win teaching, as an alternative to flip-flopping between permissiveness and the use of power, *21st Century Discipline* shows you how to:
- Elicit internally motivated cooperation
- Reinforce positive behavior without encouraging teacher-dependence
- Offer choices within limits
- Depersonalize conflicts
- Set up appropriate consequences

The layout of this book invites frequent reference, with key points printed boldly in the margins, and major concepts summarized in the form of guidelines and highlighted for quick review.

Leading Sharing Circles

This section is a thorough guide for conducting sharing circles. It covers major points to keep in mind and answers questions which will arise as you begin using the activities. Please remember that these guidelines are presented to assist you, not to restrict you. Follow them and trust your own leadership style at the same time.

Sharing Circle Procedures

1. Setting up the circle (1-2 minutes)
2. Reviewing the ground rules (1-2 minutes) *
3. Introducing the topic (1-2 minutes)
4. Sharing by circle members (12-18 minutes)
5. Reviewing what is shared (3-5 minutes) *
6. Summary discussion (2-8 minutes)
7. Closing the circle (less than 1 minute)
   *optional

Setting up the circle (1-2 minutes)

As you sit down with the children in the circle, remember that you are not teaching a lesson. You are facilitating a group of people. Establish a positive atmosphere. In a relaxed manner, address each child by name, using eye contact and conveying warmth. An attitude of seriousness blended with enthusiasm will let the children know that the sharing circle is an important learning experience—an activity that can be interesting and meaningful.

Reviewing the ground rules (1-2 minutes)

At the beginning of the first session, and at appropriate intervals thereafter, go over the ground rules for the sharing circle. They are:

Sharing Circle Rules

1. Bring yourself to the circle and nothing else.
2. Everyone gets a turn to share, including the leader.
3. You can skip your turn if you wish.
4. Listen to the person who is sharing.
5. The time is shared equally.
6. Stay in your own space.
7. There are no interruptions, probing, put-downs, or gossip.

From this point on, demonstrate to the children that you expect them to remember and abide by the ground rules. Convey that you think well of them and know they are fully capable of responsible behavior. Let them know that by coming to the session they are making a commitment to listen and show acceptance and respect for the other children and you.

Introducing the topic (1-2 minutes)

State the topic in your own words. Elaborate and provide examples as each activity suggests. Add clarifying statements of your own that will help the children understand the topic. Answer questions about the topic, and emphasize that there are no "right" responses. Finally, restate the topic, opening the session to responses (theirs and yours). Sometimes taking your turn first helps the children understand the aim of the topic. At various points throughout the session, state the topic again.

Just prior to leading a sharing circle, contemplate the topic and think of at least one possible response that *you* can make to it.

Sharing by circle members (12-18 minutes)

The most important point to remember is this: The purpose of the sharing circle is to give children an opportunity to express themselves and be accepted for the experiences, thoughts, and feelings they share. Avoid taking the action away from the circle members. They are the stars!

Reviewing what is shared (optional 3-5 minutes)

Besides modeling effective listening (the very best way to teach it) and positively reinforcing children for attentive listening, a review can be used to deliberately improve listening skills in circle members.

Reviewing is a time for reflective listening, when circle members feed back what they heard each other say during the sharing phase of the circle. Besides encouraging effective listening, reviewing provides circle members with additional recognition. It validates their experience and conveys the idea, "you are important," a message we can all profit from hearing often.

To review, a circle member simply addresses someone who shared, and briefly paraphrases what the person said ("John, I heard you say....").

The first few times you conduct reviews, stress the importance of checking with the speaker to see if the review accurately summarized the main things that were shared. If the speaker says, "No," allow him/her to make corrections. Stress too, the importance of speaking *directly* to the speaker, using the person's name and the pronoun "you," not "he" or "she." If someone says, "S/he said that...," intervene as promptly and respectfully as possible and say to the reviewer, "Talk to Betty...Say you." This is very important. The person whose turn is being reviewed will have a totally different feeling when talked *to*, instead of *about*.

Note: Remember that the review is optional and is most effective when used *occasionally*, not as a part of every circle.

Summary discussion (2-8 minutes)

The summary discussion is the cognitive portion of the sharing circle. During this phase, the leader asks thought-provoking questions to stimulate free discussion and higher-level thinking. Each sharing circle in the book includes three or more summary questions; however, at times you may want to formulate questions that are more appropriate to the level of understanding in your group—or to what was actually shared in the circle. If you wish to make connections between the sharing circle topic and a particular subject area, ask questions that will accomplish that objective and allow the summary discussion to extend longer.

It is important that you not confuse the summary with the review. The review is optional; the summary is not. The summary meets the need of people of all ages to find meaning in what they do. Thus, the summary serves as a necessary culmination to each sharing circle by allowing the children to clarify the key concepts they gained from the session.

Closing the circle (less than 1 minute)

The ideal time to end a sharing circle is when the summary discussion reaches natural closure. Sincerely thank everyone for being part of the circle. Don't thank specific students for speaking, as doing so might convey the impression that speaking is more appreciated than mere listening. Then close the circle by saying, "The sharing circle is over," or "Okay, that ends our session."

More about Sharing Circle Procedures and Rules

The next few paragraphs offer further clarification concerning sharing circle leadership.

Why should students bring themselves to the circle and nothing else? Individual teachers differ on this point, but most prefer that children not bring objects (such as pencils, books, etc.) to the circle that may be distracting.

Who gets to talk? Everyone. The importance of acceptance cannot be overly stressed. In one way or another practically every ground rule says one thing: *accept one another.* When you model acceptance of students, they will learn how to be accepting. Each individual in the circle is important and deserves a turn to speak if s/he wishes to take it. Equal opportunity to become involved should be given to everyone in the circle.

Circle members should be reinforced equally for their contributions. There are many reasons why a leader may become more enthused over what one child shares than another. The response may be more on target, reflect more depth, be more entertaining, be philosophically more in keeping with one's own point of view, and so on. However, children need to be given equal recognition for their contributions, even if the contribution is to listen silently throughout the session.

In most of the sharing circles, plan to take a turn and address the topic, too. Students usually appreciate it very much and learn a great deal when their teachers and counselors are willing to tell about their own experiences, thoughts, and feelings. In this way you let your students know that you acknowledge your own humanness.

Does everyone have to take a turn? No. Students may choose to skip their turns. If the circle becomes a pressure situation in which the members are coerced in any way to speak, it will become an unsafe place where participants are not comfortable. Meaningful discussion is unlikely in such an atmosphere. By allowing students to make this choice, you are showing them that you accept their right to remain silent if that is what they choose to do.

As you begin circles, it will be to your advantage if one or more children decline to speak. If you are unperturbed and accepting when this happens, you let them know you are offering them an opportunity to experience something you think is valuable, or at least worth a try, and not attempting to force-feed them. You as a leader should not feel compelled to share a personal experience in every session, either. However, if you decline to speak in most of the sessions, this may have an inhibiting effect on the childs' willingness to share.

A word should also be said about how this ground rule has sometimes been carried to extremes. Sometimes leaders have bent over backwards to let children know they don't have to take a turn. This seeming lack of enthusiasm on the part of the leader has caused reticence in the children. In order to avoid this outcome, don't project any personal insecurity as you lead the session. Be confident in your proven ability to work with children. Expect something to happen and it will.

Some circle leaders ask the participants to raise their hands when they wish to speak, while others simply allow free verbal sharing without soliciting the leader's permission first. Choose the procedure that works best for you, but do not call on anyone unless you can see signs of readiness.

Some leaders have reported that their first circles fell flat—that no one, or just one or two children, had anything to say. But they continued to have circles, and at a certain point everything changed. Thereafter, the children had a great deal to say that these leaders considered worth waiting for. It appears that in these cases the leaders' acceptance of the right to skip turns was a key factor. In time most children will contribute verbally when they have something they want to say, and when they are assured there is no pressure to do so.

Sometimes a silence occurs during a sharing circle. Don't feel you have to jump in every time someone stops talking. During silences children have an opportunity to think about what they would like to share or to contemplate an important idea they've heard. A general rule of thumb is to allow silence to the point that you observe group discomfort. At that point move on. *Do not switch to another topic*. To do so implies you will not be satisfied until the children speak. If you change to another topic, you are telling them you didn't really mean it when you said they didn't have to take a turn if they didn't want to.

If you are bothered about children who attend a number of circles and still do not share verbally, reevaluate what you consider to be involvement. Participation does not necessarily mean talking. Students who do not speak *are* listening and learning.

How can I encourage effective listening? The sharing circle is a time (and place) for students and leaders to strengthen the habit of listening by doing it over and over again. No one was born knowing how to listen effectively to others. It is a skill like any other that gets better as it is practiced. In the immediacy of the sharing circle, the members become keenly aware of the necessity to listen, and most children respond by expecting it of one another.

In *Creating Success,* listening is defined as the respectful focusing of attention on individual speakers. It includes eye contact with the speaker and open body posture. It eschews interruptions of any kind. When you conduct a sharing circle, listen and encourage listening in the children by (1) focusing your attention on the person who is speaking, (2) being receptive to what the speaker is saying (not mentally planning your next remark), and (3) recognizing the speaker when s/he finishes speaking, either verbally ("Thanks, Shirley") or nonverbally (a nod and a smile).

To encourage effective listening in the children, reinforce them by letting them know you have noticed they were listening to each other and you appreciate it. Occasionally conducting a review after the sharing phase also has the effect of sharpening listening skills.

How can I ensure the students get equal time? When circle members share the time equally, they demonstrate their acceptance of the notion that everyone's contribution is of equal importance. It is not uncommon to have at least one dominator in a group. This person is usually totally unaware that by continuing to talk s/he is taking time from others who are less assertive.

Be very clear with the children about the purpose of this ground rule. Tell them at the outset how much time there is and whether or not you plan to conduct a review. When it is your turn, always limit your own contribution. If someone goes on and on, do intervene (dominators need to know what they are doing), but do so as gently and respectfully as you can.

What are some examples of put-downs? Put-downs convey the message, "You are not okay as you are." Some put-downs are deliberate, but many are made unknowingly. Both kinds are undesirable in a sharing circle because they destroy the atmosphere of acceptance and disrupt the flow of discussion. Typical put-downs include:
- overquestioning.
- statements that have the effect of teaching or preaching
- advice giving
- one-upsmanship
- criticism, disapproval, or objections
- sarcasm
- statements or questions of disbelief

How can I deal with put-downs? There are two major ways for dealing with put-downs in sharing circles: preventing them from occurring and intervening when they do.

Going over the ground rules with the children at the beginning of each session, particularly in the earliest sessions, is a helpful preventive technique. Another is to reinforce the children when they adhere to the rule. Be sure to use nonpatronizing, nonevaluative language.

Unacceptable behavior should be stopped the moment it is recognized by the leader. When you become aware that a put-down is occurring, do whatever you ordinarily do to stop destructive behavior in the classroom. If one child gives another an unasked-for bit of advice, say for example, "Jane, please give Alicia a chance to tell her story." To a child who interrupts say, "Ed, it's Sally's turn." In most cases the fewer words, the better—children automatically tune out messages delivered as lectures.

Sometimes children disrupt the group by starting a private conversation with the person next to them. Touch the offender on the arm or shoulder while continuing to give eye contact to the child who is speaking. If you can't reach the offender, simply remind him/her of the rule about listening. If children persist in putting others down during sharing circles, ask to see them at another time and hold a brief one-to-one conference, urging them to follow the rules. Suggest that they reconsider their membership in the circle. Make it clear that if they don't intend to honor the ground rules, they are not to come to the circle.

How can I keep students from gossiping? Periodically remind students that using names and sharing embarrassing information is not acceptable. Urge the children to relate personally to one another, but not to tell intimate details of their lives.

What should the leader do during the summary discussion? Conduct the summary as an open forum, giving students the opportunity to discuss a variety of ideas and accept those that make sense to them. Don't impose your opinions on the children, or allow the children to impose theirs on one another. Ask open-ended questions, encourage higher-level thinking, contribute your own ideas when appropriate, and act as a facilitator.

EXPRESSING FEELINGS

Learning how to identify, accept and appropriately express our feelings is a primary quality of mental/emotional health. The activities in this section assist students to understand the function of feelings, that they are universal and how to manage them effectively.

A Time I Felt Happy —— *A Sharing Circle*

Relates to: Language Arts (oral language) K-3

> **Before introducing sharing circles to your students, please read "Leading Sharing Circles" beginning on page x.**

Objectives: The children will verbalize both positive and negative feelings.

Directions: **Review the sharing circle rules as necessary.**

State the topic. In your own words, tell the children: *Today we are going to talk about happy feelings in our sharing circle. Sometimes we feel happy and sometimes we don't—we feel unhappy. Our topic for this sharing circle is, "A Time I Felt Happy."*

Can you remember a time when you felt happy? Maybe something very nice happened and you felt good about it. Or perhaps someone did something for you that you really liked. Let's close our eyes and see if we can remember a time like that, OK? Think about it and when you look up at me, I'll know that you are ready to talk and listen. I'll say the topic again. It is, "A Time I Felt Happy."

Involve the children in sharing.

Conduct a summary. Here are two questions to ask the children. Use the questions to generate a free-flowing discussion of what was learned in the circle.
—*What did we do in this sharing circle?*
—*Why is it good for us to tell one another about times we felt happy?*

Help the children realize that they did many important things in the sharing circle. They spoke, listened, and shared feelings. Explain that in some places, like the sharing circle, it is good for people to share their feelings with one another.

Conclude the sharing circle.

A Time I Felt Unhappy — *A Sharing Circle*

Relates to: Language Arts (oral language) K-3

Objectives: | The children will verbalize both positive and negative feelings.

Directions: | **Review the sharing circle rules as necessary.**

State the topic. In your own words, tell the children *In our last sharing circle, we talked about times we felt happy. We learned that in some places, like the sharing circle, it's all right for us to tell each other about our feelings. And today we are going to do that again. Our topic for today is, "A Time I Felt Unhappy."*

Everybody feels happy at times and everybody feels unhappy at other times. It's more fun for most people to tell about happy feelings, but sometimes it does us good to talk about unhappy feelings as well. Can you remember a time when you felt unhappy? Maybe you had an accident and got hurt, or perhaps you wanted something and you didn't get it so you were disappointed. If you would like to take a turn, tell us what made you unhappy and what the feeling was like for you. Take a moment to think about it and raise your hand when you are ready. The topic is, "A Time I Felt Unhappy."

Involve the children in sharing.

Conduct a summary. Here are two questions to ask the children. Use them to generate a free flowing discussion of what was learned during the circle.
— *What did we do in this sharing circle?*
— *Why is it good for us to tell one another about times we felt unhappy?*

Conclude the sharing circle.

A Time I Felt Scared —— *A Sharing Circle*

Relates to: Language Arts (oral language) K-3

Objectives: | The children will describe emotional experiences and verbalize both positive and negative feelings.

Note: This activity is particularly effective when paired with the activity, "My Nightmare Is . . ."

Directions: | **Review the sharing circle rules as necessary.**

State the topic. Say: *Everyone feels scared from time to time and no one likes the feeling. Today, we are going to talk about feeling afraid. The topic is, "A Time I Felt Scared."*

Can you think of a time that you were afraid? What happened to cause your fear? Were you lost? Were you around a lot of people that you didn't know? Was it the first day of school? Perhaps you felt afraid the first time you tried to swim in a pool or the ocean. Chances are there is something that makes you feel scared even now. Are you afraid of the dark? Do big dogs frighten you? Maybe you feel scared when Mommy and Daddy have an argument and yell. Close your eyes and think of one time when you felt afraid. When you look up, I'll know that you are ready to begin the sharing circle. The topic is, "A Time I Felt Scared."

Involve the children in sharing.

Conduct a summary. Ask a few open-ended questions to help the children understand their thoughts about fear. For example:
— *How do we feel inside when we feel scared?*
— *What do we do sometimes when we are afraid?*
— *Why is it important to talk about our fears?*
— *How can we help each other handle our fears?*

Conclude the sharing circle.

4

My Nightmare Is . . .

Reading and Writing

Relates to: Language Arts (reading and writing) and Math (sequencing) K-3

Objectives: The children will describe emotional experiences and verbalize both positive and negative feelings.

Note: This activity is particularly effective when preceded by the sharing circle, "A Time I Felt Scared," and followed by the art activity, "Painting My Nightmare."

Time: approximately 30 minutes

Materials Needed: a copy of the book, *There's a Nightmare in My Closet*, written and illustrated by Mercer Mayer (New York, Dial Press, 1968), chalkboard, chalk, magic marker, and tagboard strips

Directions: **Read the picture book, *There's a Nightmare in My Closet*, to the children.** Show the illustrations as you read. They are large (often covering a two-page spread) and humorous. In the story, a young boy is afraid of the nightmare that is surely hiding in his bedroom closet. One night, the pajama-clad boy decides to confront the nightmare and get rid of it. A huge, cowardly monster emerges from the closet only to cry when the boy shoots him with his pop-gun. All ends well when the boy befriends the nightmare and lets it share his bed with him.

Make a story map of the sequence of events in the story. Ask the children to help. Have the children decide the four main events in the story and list them. On four separate sheets of paper draw a stick figure representation of the event in each segment. Then have the children help you arrange the pictures in sequence.

After the sequencing exercise, tell the children to think about something that makes *them* feel afraid. Say: *Remember the sharing circle, "A Time I Felt Scared." Think again about something that scares you. It can be the same thing you already shared or something different. Let's call that scary thing your "Nightmare." Think of a sentence that describes your "Nightmare." Begin your sentence, "My Nightmare is . . ."*

5

(Continued Next Page)

My Nightmare Is . . . —————— *(Continued)*

Using magic markers, write down each child's sentence on a tagboard strip—or let the child write it down. Save the "Nightmare" sentences as labels for the art activity, which follows.

Conclude the activity. Thank the children for helping you with the story map and for describing their "Nightmares" so well. Tell them that, as part of the next activity, they will get to draw pictures of their "Nightmares."

Painting My Nightmare — *An Art Activity*

Relates to: Art, K-3

Objectives:	The children will identify ways to express and deal with feelings.
Time:	approximately 30 minutes
Materials Needed:	finger paints in various colors and finger-painting paper
Directions:	**Talk to the children about Mercer Mayer's book, *There's a Nightmare in My Closet.*** Reread it and go over the story map in which the children sequenced the events of the story. Talk about the humorous Nightmare who is really a cowardly crybaby. Tell the children that they are going to paint their own "Nightmare" using finger paints. If they like, they can make it funny instead of scary. Say: *Sometimes it helps to laugh at the things that scare us. Then maybe they won't seem quite as scary.*

Have several children at a time paint their "Nightmare." Let them go to their work tables. Pour one or two of the finger paint colors on each child's paper and encourage the child to paint a funny version of his or her "Nightmare."

When the pictures are dry, let each child share his/her picture with the class. Read the sentence that the child wrote in the last activity and put it with the "Nightmare" picture.

Conclude the activity. Ask the children if they enjoyed making funny pictures of their "Nightmare." Explain that it is all right to feel afraid and that sometimes it helps to laugh about being scared.

Other books to read about fear: *Robbers, Bones and Mean Dogs,* compiled by Barry and Velma Berkey and illustrated by Marilyn Hafner (Reading, MA, Addison Wesley, 1978). In this book, children express their fears in their own words and tell about their fearful experiences. Judith Viorst's *My Mama Says There Aren't Any Zombies, Ghosts, Vampires...etc.* (New York, Atheneum, 1973). In this book, a young child lists all the "monsters" that kids are afraid of and says that his mama says positively there aren't any such things. But...mamas sometimes are wrong.

Guess the Feeling Game

Thinking and Speaking

Relates to: Language Arts (oral language) K-3

Objectives:	The children will identify ways to express and deal with feelings.
Time:	approximately 30 minutes
Materials Needed:	a copy of *I Feel* by George Ancon New York, E.P. Dutton, 1977
Directions:	**Introduce the activity.** Ask the children what kinds of feelings they experience. Describe some situations that evoke different kinds of feelings and ask the children how they would feel in those situations. For example, ask them how they would feel if they had a double-scoop ice cream cone and the ice cream fell onto the ground, or how they would feel if they made a beautiful sand castle that all the kids liked. After discussing a variety of feelings, explain that you are going to play a game with them, using a picture book about feelings.
	Read George Ancon's book, *I Feel,* to the class. It is full of large black-and-white photographs of children in situations that caused them to experience certain feelings. The word that describes the feeling expressed in a particular picture is printed in large type next to the picture. Explain to the children that they must guess what feeling each picture shows. Cover up the feeling word with your hand to hide it from those who can read. After the children guess the feeling word—or a similar word—ask if anyone will tell a little story about what is making the child in the picture feel that way. Tell the children to be detectives and to look for clues in the picture that help tell the story. Carry the game one step further and ask the children to think of what they could do to make the children with unhappy feelings feel better. Call on volunteers to share their ideas.
	Conclude the activity. Thank the children for participating, cooperating, and being good listeners. If you like, you can reward them with stickers, a hand stamp, or some other small reward.
Follow-up:	Have parent or older student volunteers read *Feelings* by Aliki (New York, Greenwillow, 1984) to small groups or single children. It is a book full of pictures, dialogues, poems, and stories about a wide range of commonly felt emotions.

A Time I Felt Excited

Relates to: Language Arts (oral language) 4-6

Objectives: The children will verbalize both positive and negative feelings and describe emotional experiences.

Directions: **Review the sharing circle rules as necessary.**

State the topic. Tell the children that this sharing circle topic is, "A Time I Felt Excited." Explain that everyone gets excited from time to time, for all kinds of reasons, but that people don't all get excited for the same reason. In your own words, say: *Different things or events make us excited. Sometimes it's a birthday, or Christmas, or another holiday, like the Fourth of July. It could be an event like a parade or a party. Does winning a game make you excited? Do you feel excited when you go on a field trip with your class or on a vacation with your family? Would it be exciting for you to go to an amusement or theme park or the zoo? Perhaps you were excited when you got a new baby brother or sister. Think about how you felt physically inside. How did you show that you were excited? Close your eyes and take a few minutes to think quietly about a time when something made you feel excited. When you look up, I'll know that you are ready to begin the circle. The topic is, "A Time I Felt Excited."*

Involve the children in sharing.

Conduct a summary. After every child in the circle has had a chance to speak, ask the children some questions to help summarize what they learned:
— *What are some of the ways we show that we are excited?*
— *Why do you think it is important to share the different things that make us excited?*
— *What kinds of things do your parents get excited about?*

Conclude the sharing circle.

Ghosts and Other Scary Creatures

Literature and Drawing

Relates to: **Language Arts (listening) and Art, 4-6**

Objectives:

The children will:
—verbalize both positive and negative feelings
—identify ways to express and deal with feelings.

Time:

45 minutes

Materials Needed:

a copy of *The Ghost-Eye Tree* by Bill Martin, Jr., and John Archambault, illustrated by Ted Rand, New York, Holt, 1985; white construction paper; and colored markers or crayons

Directions:

Introduce the activity. Begin by gathering the children around for story time. Read *The Ghost-Eye Tree*, showing the beautiful and eerie illustrations. This narrative poem tells the story of a young boy and his older sister who, while walking down a dark and lonely road on an errand for Mom one night, argue over who is afraid of the dreaded "Ghost-Eye Tree." Although the story alludes to elements of familiar fears, it is humorous and all ends well. Reread the story at least once and solicit comments from the students. Ask them why the children might have thought the tree was a ghost. Explain that it is common for children to be afraid of shadows in the dark that have scary shapes and are accompanied by frightening sounds—like the shadow of a cat in the night.

Have the children illustrate one of their *own* fears. Explain that you want them to draw the thing that scares *them* the most in the night, or at least what they imagine that thing to be. Say: *Maybe the thing that scares you is something from a bad dream, or perhaps it is something you have seen on T.V. Picture it in your mind and draw it on a piece of paper, coloring it in the scariest colors possible.*

 (Continued Next Page)

Ghosts and Other Scary Creatures —

In a second drawing, have the children "eliminate" their fear.
On a second piece of paper, invite the children to draw a picture of
the same scary thing, but this time draw it funny or pretty, or just
not frightening anymore. Talk about ways they can change the
picture to get rid of the scary parts.

**As they draw, encourage the children to talk about the scary
things in their pictures.** Praise them for their ideas, rather than
for the quality of their drawings. Ask volunteers to describe their
first drawings and how they were redrawn to eliminate the scary
parts.

Lead a discussion. When the children have finished their drawings, encourage them to talk about the experience. Use these and
other questions:
— *How did you feel about making scary things not scary
 anymore?*
— *What did it feel like to take charge over the nightmare or
 frightening object?*
— *How can we look at scary things differently—so they don't
 frighten us as much?*

Conclude the activity. Thank the children for their cooperation
and creativity.

I Felt Good and Bad About the Same Thing
_____ *A Sharing Circle*

Relates to: Language Arts (oral language) 4-6

Objectives:

The children will:
— verbalize both positive and negative feelings.
— describe emotional experiences.

Directions:

Review the sharing circle rules as necessary.

State the topic. Say to the children: *There are times when we feel good and bad about the same thing and it's confusing, so we're going to talk about times like that in our circle today. The topic is, "A Time I Felt Good and Bad About the Same Thing."*

Have you ever had to decide between two things, like which pair of shoes you would like, and then felt good about the pair you chose and bad because you didn't get the other pair? There are situations like that in which we can feel good and bad about the same thing. Think of a time when you felt good about something and bad about it too. Did you ever save some money so that you could buy a special toy? When you saved up enough and bought it you felt good, but when you spent all your money you felt bad? Perhaps you were invited to two birthday parties on the same day and you had to decide between them. You felt good that you could go to one but bad that you couldn't go to the other. Maybe you got a new baby sister and felt good about that, but when she got all the attention, you felt bad. Close your eyes for a moment and try to think of a time that you felt good and bad about the same thing. I'll know that you are ready to start when I see you looking up. The topic is, " A Time I Felt Good and Bad About the Same Thing."

Involve the children in sharing.

Conduct a summary. After all of the children have had an opportunity to speak, ask some thought-provoking questions:
— *How can something make us feel good and bad at the same time?*
— *Why do you think it is helpful to talk about both good and bad feelings?*
— *How can we have the same feelings if we all have different experiences?*

Conclude the sharing circle.

12

Feeling Mad, Sad, Bad, and Glad ──
───── Creating a Book of Poems and Photos

Relates to: Language Arts (reading and writing) 4-6

Objectives:	The children will: —verbalize both positive and negative feelings. —describe emotional experiences. —identify ways to express and deal with feelings.
Time:	two 30-minutes sessions
Materials Needed:	Ann McGovern's book, *Feeling Mad, Feeling Sad, Feeling Bad, Feeling Glad,* New York, Magic Circle Press, 1977 (or any other books of poetry about children's feelings), butcher paper, magic markers, camera with black-and-white film, pencils, and paper
Directions:	**Introduce the activity.** Read McGovern's book to the children or find other books of poetry about feelings, both good and bad. Draw a line down the center of a large piece of butcher paper and label the two columns "Good Feelings" and "Bad Feelings." Have the children brainstorm a list of feeling words and write them in the appropriate columns on the paper. After filling both columns with feeling words, explain to the children that they will have an opportunity to become authors of a class book on feelings.

Explain to your students that you want them to choose two feelings—one good and one bad— and write a poem about each. Afterwards, they will be able to "pose" for two photographs, one to illustrate each poem. Reassure the children about the ease of the task by saying: *Your poems do not have to rhyme. They can simply be special ways of describing how things, like a lost dog or a tray of cookies, make you feel. This will be a special book in two ways: First, you will be the authors, and second, you will be in the pictures.*

Share the poems. When they are finished writing, ask the children to read their poems to a partner or a "read-around" group of four or five children for suggestions. Encourage revisions and the use of colorful and descriptive words. Collect the poems to save them for rewriting on good paper and insertion into the book.

 (Continued Next Page)

Take the photographs. Ask the children to think of ways to pose for a picture to illustrate each poem. Suggest that they show the feeling in their faces or use props from around the room. Take two pictures of each child, one showing the good feeling and one showing the bad.

When the pictures are developed, have a book-constructing session. Ask the children to rewrite each poem at the top of a good piece of paper. Give them the photograph to glue on the same paper, under the poem. Brainstorm ideas for a book title and let a volunteer make a cover for the book, using tagboard or construction paper. Have the volunteer write the title and draw an illustration on the cover. Let another child make a table of contents to help locate the poems and authors. Bind the poems between the front and back covers, using a hole puncher and rings, staples, or any other kind of binder to which you have access.

Conclude the activity. Let the children look through the book, and display it for an open-house or PTA meeting. Another option is to let the children take turns borrowing the book for one night so that they can share it with their families. Ask the children how they feel about being the authors of their own books, and thank them for contributing.

Feeling Mobiles

Craft Project and Discussion

Relates to: Language Arts (oral and written language) and Art, 4-6

Objectives: The children will:
— verbalize both positive and negative feelings.
— identify ways to express and deal with feelings.
— identify and select appropriate behaviors to specific emotional situations.

Time: approximately 20 to 30 minutes

Materials Needed: wire hangers for every two students in the class; magazines with pictures (optional), construction paper in various colors, colored index cards (3-inch by 5-inch), varied lengths of colored yarn (or string), crayons or marking pens, and prepared slips of paper with feeling-words written on them

Directions: **Preparation:** On each of several small slips of paper (one for every two students), write a feeling word, like disappointment, anger, jealousy, joy, frustration, happiness, sadness, curiosity, fear, confusion, excitement, surprise, embarrassment, shame, loneliness, disgust, etc. You may repeat words. Place the slips of paper in a box or other container.

Ask the children to choose partners. Explain that each pair of students will design a mobile using a specific feeling as the theme. Have each pair draw a slip of paper from the box.

Distribute the materials and explain the procedure. Say to the children: *The hanger is the frame from which you will string pictures, sayings, words, or stories that define your feeling. First, brainstorm as many ideas as you can about your feeling word. Then decide what pictures, sayings, and shapes best depict those ideas. You may use symbols or exact definitions and images. String each picture, shape, symbol, color, or phrase separately with a different length of yarn. The mobile should show others how you define different aspects of your feeling word.*

15

(Continued Next Page)

When the mobiles are finished, hang them from lighting fixtures, or from wire or clothesline stretched across the room.

Have the children share their mobiles. Have the class focus on one mobile at a time, while its designers talk about the feeling it is intended to depict, and the items they chose to symbolize that feeling. Ask these and other questions:
— *Why did you choose these colors?*
— *What phrases or sayings come to mind when you think of this feeling?*
— *What, if any, universal symbols does society use to define the feeling?*
— *Are there universal ways of expressing the feeling? What are they?*

Conclude the activity. Thank the children for their thoughtful and creative depictions of the feeling words.

Booster Statements

Experience Sheet and Discussion

Relates to: **Language Arts (oral and written language) 4-6**

Objectives:

The children will:
— verbalize both positive and negative feelings.
— identify and select appropriate behaviors to specific emotional situations.

Note: This is the first in a sequence of two activities having to do with giving and receiving positive comments. It should precede the activity, "Booster-Talk Goals."

Time:

approximately 25 to 30 minutes

Materials Needed:

one copy of the experience sheet, "Booster Statements" for each child; large sheets of newsprint and marking pen

Directions:

Distribute the experience sheets and explain the activity. Tell the children that the experience sheet is intended to help the class examine the kinds of communication that can help people to feel good about themselves.

Review the directions. Say to the children: *Write down the exact words that would make you feel good about yourself. Be specific. For example, instead of writing, "I feel good when Dad gives me a compliment," write "Dad told me he was proud of me for the 'A' I got in Math."*

Collect the experience sheets. On four separate sheets of newsprint or butcher paper, write the headings, "Friend," "Mom/Dad," "Teacher/Counselor," and "YOU." Go through the experience sheets and record several booster statements in each of the four categories.

 (Continued Next Page)

Booster Statements

Discuss the booster statements with the students. Ask these and other open-ended questions:

— *What are the major differences among the statements?*

— *Would anyone not feel good hearing these words said to him or her?*

— *Are there some statements here that might be considered insincere?*

— *How can you tell when a statement is sincere? ...insincere?*

— *Why is it sometimes difficult for us to receive compliments ?*

— *How do you feel when you are given a compliment that you think you don't deserve?*

Conclude the activity. Suggest that the children notice how they feel when they receive booster statements in the future, and how other people react when they receive them. Thank the children for their contributions. Post the booster statements around the room.

Booster Statements

DO NOT WRITE YOUR NAME ON THIS SHEET

Directions: On the lines below, write down the *exact words* that these people could say to you that would make you feel happy, proud, or important.

1. A friend:

_____

_____

2. Your Mom or Dad:

_____

_____

3. Your teacher or counselor:

_____

_____

4. Now write down <u>two things</u> that you could say *to yourself*:

_____

_____

_____

Booster-Talk Goals ———————

Experience Sheet and Discussion

Relates to: Language Arts (oral language) 4-6

Objectives:

The children will:
— verbalize both positive and negative feelings.
— identify and select appropriate behaviors to specific emotional situations.
— make positive statements about self and others.
— identify ways to express and deal with feelings.

Note: This is the second in a sequence of two activities having to do with giving and receiving positive comments. It should be preceded by the activity, "Booster Statements."

Time:

approximately 15 to 20 minutes on two separate days about one week apart

Materials Needed:

one copy of the experience sheet, "Booster-Talk Goals," for each child; a large envelope, tape or stapler, and the lists of booster words (from the previous activity) posted around the room

Directions:

Distribute the experience sheets. Explain that each student will be conducting his or her own personal experiment in human behavior.

Go over the directions on the experience sheet. Say to the children: *Choose three people that you can honestly say something nice to. Record the names of the people in the appropriate spaces and write out the exact words that you will say to them. Select words from the booster sheets posted around the room or use your own words. Set a deadline for each experiment and write it down, too. Try to complete all three of your experiments by* <u>one week from today</u>.

Allow time for the students to complete the experience sheets. Then instruct them to fold and staple or tape their sheet closed and write their name on the outside of it.

Collect the sheets and place them in the large envelope and seal it. Place the envelope in a safe place. One week later, return the sheets and allow the students to complete them.

(Continued Next Page)

Lead a culminating discussion. Invite the children to talk about their experiences. Ask these and other open-ended questions:
— *What happened when you delivered each of your positive messages?*
— *How did the person react to your statement?*
— *How did you feel before you made the statement?*
— *How did you feel after making the statement?*
— *What was the best part of the experiment?*
— *What did you learn from this exercise?*

Conclude the activity. Thank the children for their participation. *Do not recollect the experience sheets.*

Extension: Repeat the experiment periodically throughout the year.

Booster-Talk Goals

Directions: Think of three people to whom you would like to say something nice. They can be people in your class, your Mom, Dad, brother, sister, neighbor, teacher, or anyone else.

Keeping those three people in mind, complete the *left* side of the sheet below. Then fold your paper in half and write your name on the outside. Place your paper in the large envelope.

In a few days, your goal sheet will be handed back to you. At that time, fill in the *right* side of the paper. No one will be permitted to look at your sheet. You do not have to tell anyone what your goals are.

Goal 1: I will try saying something nice

to_____.

This is what I will say: _____

_____

_____

_____

by _____
　　　　　　　　date

Result 1: I completed my goal

_____yes _____no

After I said something nice, the person

said to me:_____

_____

_____

Goal 2: I will try saying something nice

to_____.

This is what I will say: _____

_____

_____

_____

by _____
　　　　　　　　date

Result 2: I completed my goal

_____yes _____no

After I said something nice, the person

said to me:_____

_____

_____

Goal 3: I will try saying something nice

to_____.

This is what I will say: _____

_____

_____

_____

by _____
　　　　　　　　date

Result 3: I completed my goal

_____yes _____no

After I said something nice, the person

said to me:_____

_____

_____

A Time I Handled My Feelings Well —

A Sharing Circle

Relates to: Language Arts (oral language) 4-6

Objectives:

The children will:
—identify ways to express and deal with feelings.
—demonstrate a positive attitude about self.

Directions:

Review the sharing circle rules as necessary.

State the topic. Say to the children: *Sometimes we face situations that cause us to experience strong feelings. How we behave at those times depends on how well we take charge of our feelings. Today, we're going to talk about instances when the outcome was good. Our topic is, "A Time I Handled My Feelings Well."*

For example, maybe you wanted a special gift for your birthday or Christmas and didn't receive it because your parents either failed to realize how important it was to you or couldn't afford it. Since you didn't want to hurt their feelings, you didn't express your disappointment to them, but told a friend instead. Perhaps you were very angry at someone and wanted to hit the person, but instead managed to talk to him or her and express your angry feelings without hitting. Maybe you lost a game or an election and really wanted to yell, but instead congratulated the winner. Possibly you injured yourself and it hurt so badly that you needed to cry, so you did. Handling your feelings well usually means doing what is appropriate, without hurting someone else in the process. Think of a situation that you feel OK sharing. When you are ready, raise your hand. The topic is, "A Time I Handled My Feelings Well."

Involve the children in sharing.

Conduct a summary. Ask several open-ended questions to generate a discussion:
— *What similarities were there in the ways we handled our feelings?*
— *What differences were there?*
— *If our feelings are always acceptable, why isn't our behavior always acceptable?*
— *What do we have to control, our feelings or our behavior? How can we do that?*

Conclude the sharing circle.

23

DEVELOPING
SELF AWARENESS

When we are aware that we experience feelings, thoughts and behavior, our self-understanding increases. As we become aware that others experience feelings, thoughts and behavior, our understanding of others increases. When we understand that we are like others in this way, our respect for both ourselves and others increases. The activities in this section help students focus on and understand their experiences of feeling, thinking, and behaving, and how these experiences interrelate.

Something I Like About Myself

A Sharing Circle

Language Arts (oral language) K-3

Objectives:

The children will:
—demonstrate a positive attitude about self.
—describe positive characteristics about self.

Directions:

Review the sharing circle rules as necessary.

Introduce the topic: In your own words, say to the children: *Today we are going to talk about something everybody loves to talk about. We will talk about ourselves! We're going to get a chance to say some very good and true things about ourselves. The topic is, "Something I Like about Myself."*

Think about yourself for a few moments. You have so many good qualities that it may be hard to decide which one to talk about. Maybe you're glad to be yourself because you learn things so easily. Or maybe you are good at playing and having fun with your friends. Perhaps you like something about your body, like your curly hair or your freckles. Maybe you're proud of your ability to play games and sports well. Let's think about it for a moment. When you are ready to share, raise your hand. The topic is, "Something I Like about Myself."

Involve the children in sharing.

Conduct a summary. Ask these and other questions to stimulate a free-flowing discussion:
—*Is it okay for us to say what we like about ourselves in the sharing circle?*
—*Why is it good for us to take pride in ourselves?*
—*How do other people let you know that they are proud of you?*

Assure the children that the sharing circle is a perfect place for them to say positive things about themselves. Help them to articulate how important it is to like and take pride in themselves.

Conclude the sharing circle.

Something I Really Like To Do at School ———————— A Sharing Circle

Relates to: Language Arts (oral language) K-3

Objectives: The children will identify interests, abilities, strengths, and weaknesses as components of personal uniqueness.

Directions: **Review the sharing circle rules as necessary.**

State the topic. In your own words, tell the children, *Our topic for this sharing circle is, "Something I Really Like To Do at School." There are so many enjoyable things we do at school. I like practically everything we do, but I do have some favorites. Today I'd like you to think about what you enjoy most here at school. Perhaps you like games because you like moving your body. Maybe you are very good at learning to read. Or perhaps you enjoy our sharing circles most because you get to talk and tell us what's on your mind. Think it over for a few moments and when you are ready to begin, look up at me. The topic is, "Something I Really Like To Do at School."*

Involve the children in sharing.

Conduct a summary. Ask these and other questions to stimulate a free-flowing discussion:
—*What are some of the things we like to do here at school?*
—*Is it okay if the thing you like to do is different from the things others like to do?*

Conclude the sharing circle.

How My Mistake Helped Me Learn ——

—————————————— *A Sharing Circle*

Relates to: Language Arts (oral language) K-3

Objectives: | The children will describe mistakes they've made and what they learned from those mistakes.

Directions: | **Review the sharing circle rules as necessary.**

State the topic. Say to the children: *When we make choices, we sometimes choose the wrong thing. We call this making a mistake. Our topic today is, "How My Mistake Helped Me Learn."*

We all make mistakes—and we all have a chance to learn something from every mistake we make. Mistakes are like good friends—they teach us things we need to know. Think of a mistake you *made that taught you something. It can be a big mistake, or a small one. For example, maybe you tried to spell a new word and used the wrong letter, but making that mistake helped you learn to spell the word correctly. Or maybe you asked for a great big piece of cake with ice cream, and when your stomach hurt afterwards, you learned not to take so much next time. Perhaps you wandered off in the shopping center and lost your parents for awhile. How did you find them again, and what did you learn? Maybe you left your bike outside overnight and in the morning it was gone. What did that mistake teach you? Think quietly for a few minutes. Think of a mistake you made, and then think about what you learned from making it. Raise your hand when you're ready to share. The topic is, "How My Mistake Helped Me Learn."*

Involve the children in sharing.

Conduct a summary. Ask these and other questions to help the children summarize what they have learned:
—*Does everyone make mistakes?*
—*Is it OK to make mistakes?*
—*What can mistakes teach us about ourselves?*
—*If we let them, can mistakes be our friends? How?*

Conclude the sharing circle.

A Time I Had Fun with a Friend

A Sharing Circle

Relates to: Language Arts (oral language) K-3

Objectives: The children will describe leisure activities and will identify the value of sharing enjoyable activities with friends.

Directions: **Review the sharing circle rules as necessary.**

Introduce the topic. Say to the children: *We all have work to do, both at home and at school. Work is important. But fun and play are important too. Today we're going to talk about having fun. Our topic is, "A Time I Had Fun with a Friend."*

Think of something fun that you did with a friend. Maybe you and your friend went to a movie together—or to Disney World. Perhaps you played dress-up together, or hide-and-seek. Or maybe you went to your friend's house and played in the bedroom with his or her toys. Did you share an ice cream with your friend after school? Did you play a video or computer game together? Take a few minutes to think of something you did with a friend that you enjoyed. Raise your hand when you are ready to speak. Our topic is, "A Time I Had Fun with a Friend."

Involve the children in sharing.

Conduct a summary. Generate a free-flowing discussion by asking these and other questions:
— *What kinds of fun things do we do with our friends?*
— *Do our friends have fun doing those things too?*
— *How can you tell if a person is having fun?*
— *Why is it important to do enjoyable things when we're not working?*
— *What would it be like if we worked all the time and never had fun?*

Conclude the sharing circle.

One of the Best Times I Ever Had with My Family ———— *A Sharing Circle*

Relates to: Language Arts (oral language) 4-6

Objectives:

The children will:
—describe leisure activities pursued by family and self.
—identify the value of leisure activities to self.

Directions:

Review the sharing circle rules as necessary.

State the topic. Say to the children: *Our topic today is, "One of the Best Times I Ever Had With My Family." Think about a time when you were with one or more members of your family and everyone had a particularly enjoyable time together. Maybe you visited a roller rink or an amusement park, or took a family trip to a special place. Perhaps you were celebrating someone's birthday, or maybe you all just decided to go to a movie together. Tell us what you did with your family, and tell us what made it so enjoyable. Think about it for a moment, and raise your hand when you are ready to share. Today's topic is, "One of the Best Times I Ever Had With My Family."*

Involve the children in sharing.

Conduct a summary. After all of the children who want to share have had a turn, ask questions such as these:
— *How did you feel when you went (horseback riding with your family)?*
— *How did other members of your family seem to feel?*
— *Did all of us get the same feelings in the same ways when we had good times with our families?*
— *What differences in feelings and experiences did you notice?*
— *Why is it important to have good times with our families?*

Conclude the sharing circle.

My Circle of Friends and Family

Experience Sheet and Discussion

Relates to: **Language Arts (reading and writing) 4-6**

Objective:	The children will describe leisure activities pursued by family, self, and friends.
Time:	approximately 20 to 30 minutes
Materials Needed:	one copy of the experience sheet, "This Is My Circle of Friends and Family," for each child; art and writing materials for the children; chart paper and magic marker
Directions:	**Introduce the activity.** Distribute the experience sheets. Read the directions at the top of the experience sheet—or ask a volunteer to read them to the rest of the class. If you like, fill out an experience sheet yourself in advance and read several of your own entries to help clarify the task. Stress that you want the children to think about positive things that people like to do.

Have the children complete the experience sheet. If you like, ask them to work in small groups. This will encourage them to help one another focus on the likes and hobbies of their friends and families. While the children are working, circulate and offer help and suggestions, as needed.

Conduct a follow-up discussion. When the children have completed their experience sheets, ask volunteers to each share one thing that a friend or family member likes to do. Then ask several culminating discussion questions, such as these:
—*Do we all have certain things that we like to do?*
—*Do we all enjoy doing the same things?*
—*Why do you think it's important to do things that we like to do?*

Conclude the activity. Thank the children for their participation and cooperation.

This Is My Circle of Friends and Family

1. Write the names of your friends and family members on the lines provided around the outside of the circle.

2. Draw *yourself* on the figure without a face. Add *your* name to that line.

3. Under each name, write one or more words that describe something that person likes to do. Under your own name, write something that *you* like to do.

Achievement Time Capsule

Art, Collection, and Discussion

Relates to: **Art and Language Arts (oral language) 4-6**

Objectives: The children will describe personal successes and achievements.

Time: approximately 45 minutes

Materials Needed: one shoe box and a collection of awards and/or symbols of achievement for each child; magazines, scissors, and glue

Directions: **Introduce the activity.** Tell the children that each of them is going to have an opportunity to create a time capsule. Explain that a time capsule is a container that holds things representing a particular period in time. Time capsules are usually sealed and stored, and are not opened again for many years. Say to the children: *This time capsule will be an <u>achievement</u> time capsule. It will remind you of your achievements at home, school, church, or in the community this year. In the time capsule, place ribbons, awards, report cards, "A" tests, programs from plays you performed in, or photographs that show you achieving something special, like diving into a pool or doing a pull-up. You might even include drawings that represent certain achievements, like planting a garden. Continue to put things into your time capsule throughout the year. At the end of the year, put the capsule away. When you open it again sometime in the future, you'll be pleased to have so many examples of your achievements.*

Distribute the materials and explain the procedure. Say to the children: *The shoe box will become your time capsule. Decorate it with pictures from magazines. Choose pictures that represent <u>future</u> achievements. For example, if you want to become a veterinarian someday, cut out pictures of animals and paste them all over the box. If you want to achieve in sports, decorate your capsule with sports pictures. Choose a variety of pictures to represent interests, future goals, or desired achievements.*

 (Continued Next Page)

Achievement Time Capsule

Have a sharing session. After clean-up, invite the children to share their achievement time capsules with the class. Ask them to explain why they chose certain pictures to decorate their capsule. Ask them what awards and symbols of achievement they plan to put into the time capsule during the year. Talk about the effort that will be required to realize their goals and desired achievements.

Lead a summary discussion. Ask these and other open-ended questions:
— *Why do you think it is important to talk about desired achievements?*
— *How do you feel when you achieve something?*
— *Why is it important to remember our special achievements?*

Conclude the activity. Thank the children for sharing and suggest that they keep their time capsules in a safe place at home, continuing to add items throughout the year

A Time I Made a Big Effort and Succeeded ————— A Sharing Circle

Relates to: Language Arts (oral language) 4-6

Objectives: The children will describe behaviors that led to a successful experience.

Directions: **Review the sharing circle rules as necessary.**

State the topic. Say to the children: *Today we're going to talk about what it's like to accomplish something after trying very hard. Our topic is, "A Time I Made a Big Effort and Succeeded."*

Have you ever tried very hard to do something and finally succeeded? Perhaps you worked hard to write a story, changing words around to make it sound better and adding descriptions and action verbs, and finally finishing a good copy that you were proud of. Maybe you practiced running everyday until you ran a mile without stopping. Or perhaps you planted a garden, watering and weeding it regularly. At last you were rewarded by beautiful flowers or delicious vegetables. Have you ever worked many hours to make a model or build something, like a fort? How did you feel about succeeding after having made such a big effort? Were you proud of yourself? Did you feel good? Take a few moments to think about it before we begin. Our circle topic is, "A Time I Made a Big Effort and Succeeded."

Involve the children in sharing.

Conduct a summary. When every child has had an opportunity to speak, ask the children some questions to stimulate their thinking:
— *How did we feel about succeeding after making a big effort?*
— *Why is it important to keep trying even when something is difficult?*
— *What is the difference between making a big effort and just wishing for something to happen?*
— *What did you learn about yourself from this activity?*

Conclude the sharing circle.

Winning Qualities

Experience Sheet and Discussion in Triads

Relates to: **Language Arts (writing and oral language) 4-6**

Objectives:

The children will:
— describe positive characteristics about self as perceived by self and others.
— demonstrate a positive attitude about self.
— identify interests, abilities, and strengths as components of personal uniqueness.

Time:

approximately 30 minutes

Materials Needed:

a pencil and one copy of the experience sheet, "Winning Qualities: Write a Sentence About Yourself!" for each child

Directions:

Distribute the experience sheets to the children. Read the directions at the top of the experience sheet. Tell the children that they will have 10 minutes to complete it. Explain that they will then have the opportunity to share their sentences with two class-mates.

Have the children begin filling out the experience sheet. Circulate and lend assistance, as needed.

Ask the children to share, in triads. Designate groups of three children who are already seated near one another and who get along well. Tell the children to take turns reading their sentences. Allow about two minutes per child.

Lead a culminating discussion. When the triad discussions are complete, gather the group together and ask these and other open-ended questions:
— *How does it feel to talk about yourself this way to others?*
— *Why is it good to say nice things about ourselves?*
— *Why do you think it feels strange to complement yourself?*

Conclude the activity. Affirm the importance of knowing what one's "winning qualities" are. Thank the children for their cooperation and participation.

Winning Qualities:
Write a Sentence about Yourself!

Here are three lists of words. On each list, check the words that describe you best, or write a word or two of your own on each list.

1. Adjective (pick 2)

___ friendly
___ polite
___ honest
___ dependable
___ cooperative
___ creative
___ enthusiastic
___ smart

___ _____

___ _____

2. Noun (pick 1)

___ student
___ boy
___ girl
___ person
___ friend

___ _____

___ _____

___ _____

___ _____

3. Action verb (pick 2)

___ enjoys other people
___ works hard
___ achieves well in school
___ gets along well with others
___ is fun to be with
___ has good ideas

___ learns quickly
___ is good at _____
___ is great at _____

___ _____

___ _____

Now, write a sentence that describes you. Write the words you checked in the blanks, as shown:

I am a _____ and _____
　　　　　　(from list 1)　　　　　　　　　　　　　　　　(from list 1)

_____ who _____
　　　(from list 2)　　　　　　　　　　　　　(from list 3)

and _____.
　　　　　(from list 3)

DEALING WITH STRESS

This section focuses student attention on the fundamental importance of physical, mental and emotional health as it creates an understanding of the role of stress in their lives. It provides important information and activities that encourage students to take conscious control of their own wellness.

Healthy Food I Like —————————

————————— *Discussion and Food Preparation*

Relates to: Language Arts (oral language)
Health, Science, and Math, K-3

Objectives: | The children will describe how having healthy eating habits can reduce stress.

Time: | 15 to 20 minutes

Materials Needed: | a variety of vegetables that can be cut up and eaten raw (cucumber, carrot, celery, zucchini, jicama, red cabbage, etc.), a paring knife, small paper plates, napkins, butcher paper, magic marker, scissors, and clothespins

Directions: | **Introduce the activity.** Ask the children to raise their hands if they remember a time when they were sick or not feeling well. Ask them if they felt like working or playing when they were sick. Explain that even adults don't want to work or play when they are sick. On chart paper, create a "mind map" showing several different ways the children can keep themselves healthy. Write the word "health" in the center of the paper and plot each idea as a "branch" emanating from that central theme. Use both words and symbols. Include ideas like personal hygiene, getting plenty of rest and exercise, talking about feelings, and eating good foods. Say to them: *We are going to have an opportunity to try some nutritious foods to find out if we like them or not. Today we will be taste testers and sample some vegetables.*

Using the magic markers, butcher paper, and scissors, draw and cut out a T-graph for each vegetable to be "tested." Each T should be 12 inches wide at the crossbar and 18 inches tall. Draw around the outside of the T, making both the crossbar and the stem about 2 1/2 to 3 inches thick. Within either end of the T-graph crossbar, draw a happy face with the word "yes," and a sad face with the word "no." Across the top of the T-bar, write the words, "Do you like . . .," with a picture of the vegetable. (When you cut out the T-bar, allow extra paper along the top edge for both the words and drawing—on all other edges, cut along the lines).

(Continued Next Page)

Healthy Food I Like ————————— *(Continued)*

Introduce the vegetables to the children and talk about where each comes from and how it is grown. Then place the T-graphs at separate stations around the room. At each station place a pile of clothespins, a whole sample of the vegetable for the children to examine, and many bite-size pieces for them to taste.

Divide the children into small groups and send a group to each station. Tell them: *After you have examined the vegetable, take a sample and taste it. If you like it, clip a clothespin to the stem of the T-bar under the happy face. If you don't like it, clip a clothes-pin under the sad face.*

If you have enough samples and clothespins, have the groups rotate and try some other vegetables.

Tally and compare the vegetable "votes." Gather the children together and ask them these and other questions to generate a discussion:
— *Which vegetable(s) did you like most?*
— *Which vegetable(s) did you like least?*
— *Did anyone discover a vegetable that you'd like to eat more of at home?*
— *Why is it important to eat vegetables?*
—*How can healthful eating help relieve stress?*

Ask the children to help sequence the vegetable samples from "most liked" to "least liked." Or simply divide them into "most liked" and "least liked" groups.

Conclude the activity. Thank the children for being such good taste testers.

Extension:

Taste test different fruits on another day and several breads on yet another. Show the children that there are many delicious foods that are good for the body.

How I Keep Myself Well

A Sharing Circle

Relates to: Art and Language Arts (oral language) K-3

Objectives: The children will:
—demonstrate knowledge of good health habits.
—describe how healthful eating habits can relieve stress.

Directions: **Review the sharing circle rulesas necessary.**

State the topic. Say to the children: *We all like to feel well and have lots of energy. It's no fun to be sick. Today's topic is "How I Keep Myself Well."*

Sometimes we can't help it when we get sick, but we can do some things to keep ourselves as healthy as possible. Think of something that you do to keep yourself well. Perhaps you wash your hands with soap and water to get the germs off after you use the bathroom. Maybe you eat lots of fruits and vegetables and not very many sweets. Do you brush your teeth after you eat? That's one way you can take care of your health. Do you tell your parents or teacher if you have any pains inside? That's important. Maybe you take a bath or shower everyday. Keeping clean helps you stay healthy. So does exercising when you feel mad inside. Close your eyes for a few moments and think about what you do to keep yourself well. When you have thought of something, open your eyes—then I'll know that you are ready to begin the circle. The topic is, "How I Keep Myself Well."

Involve the children in sharing.

Conduct a summary. When every child in the circle has had a chance to speak, ask the children some questions to help summarize what they have learned:
—*In what ways do we keep ourselves healthy?*
—*Why do you think it is helpful to talk about how we keep ourselves well?*
—*How can we learn more about staying healthy and stress free?*

Conclude the sharing circle.

Movement Can Reduce Stress

Movement and Discussion

Relates to: Social Studies, Physical Education, and Language Arts, K-3

Objectives: The children will demonstrate healthful ways of coping with conflicts, stress, and emotions.

Time: approximately 15 to 20 minutes

Directions: **Begin this activity with a discussion of how the children feel when they are angry or upset and these emotions build up inside them.** Ask them to describe how they feel physically. Suggest to them: *Maybe you get a headache or become grouchy, even with friends. Or perhaps your neck and shoulders ache. Letting negative feelings build up inside us is kind of like shaking a can of soda. The gas bubbles build up and want to come out. When we are feeling mad and upset, we may strike out verbally or physically to release all that negative energy. Then people get hurt.*

Ask the children to suggest ways that they can physically *use* that energy to release the tension that builds up inside; for example, through sports, exercise, singing, and dancing. Tell the children that you are going to lead them through some movement activities that will help release built-up energy.

Go outdoors or use a auditorium where there is plenty of space. Ask the children to form several rows. Direct the rows to stand far enough apart to allow for plenty of movement.

Ask the children to copy your movements. Begin by stretching: arms, hands, legs, neck, torso. Then begin waving arms, head, legs (one at a time or lie down and wave both at once). Next, stand up and begin running in place. Then add arm-shaking and body-wiggling while running. Tell the children that they are shaking out a lot of the built-up stress and tension.

43

(Continued Next Page)

Movement Can Reduce Stress

Continue the total-group exercises for about 5 to 7 minutes.
Then invite the children to choose a partner. Have one child lead
movements while the other copies. Allow 2 to 3 minutes for this.
Then ask the children to switch roles and continue the activity.

Lead a discussion. After the activity, ask a few open-ended
questions like these:
— *How did it feel to put your energy into exercising?*
— *Why do you think it helps to do something physically active
when you are experiencing anger, tension, or other negative
feelings?*
— *How can you use these ideas when you are upset at home? In
school?*

Conclude the activity. Help the children formulate some statements about the benefits of physical activity and laughter in
releasing stress. Have the children write these on sentence strips
and post them around the room.

Recognizing Peer Pressure

Brainstorming and Discussion

Relates to: Language Arts (reading and listening) K-3

Objectives: The children will:
—describe peer pressure as a source of stress.
—identify types of peer pressure and their effects.

Time: approximately 30 minutes

Materials Needed: chalkboard and chalk or chart paper and magic marker

Directions: **Write the heading "Peer Pressure" on the chalkboard or chart paper.** Gather the children together and, in your own words, define the term. For example, say: *A **peer** is someone who is like you in many ways. Your peers are about the same age as you are, they go to school like you do, and they like many of the same things that you like. The other children in this class are your peers. My peers are other adults who went to college and have jobs. For example, the principal and the other teachers in this school are my peers.*

*Pressure is a type of force. For instance, when I push this door open, or close this drawer, I do it with the pressure of my hand (demonstrate). That's a type of physical pressure. The kind of pressure we're going to talk about today, however, is not physical. Instead, it comes from the **words** and **actions** of other people. Peer pressure comes from the words and actions of your peers. If someone in this class tries to get you to do something that you don't want to do, that's an example of peer pressure. If your friend tries to get you to do something you might want to do, but aren't sure about, that's peer pressure, too. Sometimes peer pressure is good, and sometimes it's harmful. Peer pressure is good when it makes us consider things that are good for us—like being friendly or playing fair. Peer pressure is harmful when it tries to get us to do something that is wrong or unhealthy.*

(Continued Next Page)

Recognizing Peer Pressure — *(Continued)*

Write the following (or another) example on the board or chart:

• Billy is supposed to go to the library after school and pick out some books. Ted and Jeff try to convince him to play catch instead.

Discuss the example with the children. Use these and other open-ended questions:

— *Is this an example of good peer pressure or harmful peer pressure?*

— *If Billy says no, and the other boys accept his answer, is it still peer pressure?*

— *How do you think Billy feels when his friends try to get him to do something he's not supposed to do?*

— *What could happen if Billy gives in and plays catch instead of going to the library?*

— *What could happen if Billy refuses to play with his friends?*

— *What would you say if you were Billy? What would you do? What might happen if you said/did that?*

One at a time, list and discuss other examples of peer pressure. Use some of your own, ask the children to contribute some, or use the examples listed on the following page. Discuss each one with the children, asking open-ended questions (like those above) tailored to the example. When the children suggest ways of responding to a harmful pressure situation, write them down on the chart. Discuss how well each suggestion would work.

(Continued Next Page)

Recognizing Peer Pressure — *(Continued)*

Peer-Pressure Situations:

- Mary wants to copy Angela's answers on a test.

- Dennis tries to get Bruce to get up earlier, so he won't be late for school.

- Molly wants Chris to ride his bike with her to the park on a other side of town, even though his parents told him not to ride that far.

- John wants David to smoke a cigarette.

- Judy tries to convince Michael to use hand signals when he rides his bike.

- Kelly urges Melinda to wear her mother's pearl necklace—without permission.

- Paul tries to convince Tammy that school is boring and she shouldn't study so much.

- Jean and Lita think Janice is weird and urge Diane not to talk to her.

- Diane urges Jean and Lita to invite Janice to play with them.

- Joey tells Manny that boys shouldn't have teddybears and urges Manny to throw his in the dumpster.

Conclude the activity. Emphasize that peer-pressure situations can take many forms, both good and harmful. It is important to recognize harmful peer pressure situations and know how to handle them. Thank the children for their suggestions and participation

Four Ways to Say No

Role Playing and Discussion

Relates to: **Drama and Language Arts (listening and speaking) K-3**

Objectives:	The children will: — identify sources and effects of peer pressure. — demonstrate appropriate behaviors when peer pressure is contrary to one's beliefs. **Note:** This activity should be preceded by the brainstorming and discussion activity, "Recognizing Peer Pressure."
Time:	approximately 30 to 40 minutes (may be done in two 15- to 20-minute sessions)
Materials Needed:	examples of harmful peer pressure situations from the previous activity, chart paper, and magic marker
Directions:	**Introduce the activity.** Remind the children of the term *peer pressure*, and ask them if they can remember what it means. Review the definition, and talk briefly about the differences between good and harmful peer pressure. Say: *Today we're going to learn and practice four different ways to handle peer pressure when we think it could be harmful.* **Pick one of the examples that you and the children talked about in the previous activity, such as:** • Molly wants Chris to ride his bike with her to the park on a other side of town, even though his parents told him not to ride that far. **Ask two children to come forward and play the parts of Molly and Chris.** Direct "Molly" to try to urge "Chris" to ride to the park with her. Tell Chris to simply say, "no." • Write the words <u>**Say no**</u> in large letters on the chart paper.

48   (Continued Next Page)

Allow the children to act out the situation for a few moments, then stop the action. Suggest that Molly *not* take no for an answer. Direct her to keep pressuring Chris. This time, tell Chris to say, "no," and suggest that they do something else, such as "ride to the corner store and get an ice cream."

• Write the words **<u>Say No, and suggest something else to do</u>** on the chart.

Allow a few more moments of role-playing, then stop the action again. Tell Molly to keep up the pressure, and direct Chris to say, "no," and give a reason, such as, "my parents don't think it's safe for me to ride that far."

• On the chart, write the words, **<u>Say no, and give a reason</u>**.

Allow the children to act out this exchange, before stopping the action once more. Tell Molly not to give up, but this time tell Chris to say, "no," and walk away.

• On the chart, write the words, **<u>Say no, and leave</u>**.

Have the children act out the fourth and final strategy, which will end the role play.

Review the strategies. At the top of the chart, write the heading "Four Ways to Say No." Ask the children to read the four strategies with you. Explain that in potentially harmful peer-pressure situations, they should remember these four strategies. Tell them: *If the first doesn't work, use the second. If the second doesn't work, use the third. If the third doesn't work, use the fourth— leave the situation.*

Have the children role play additional examples of harmful peer pressure. Act out one example at a time in front of the rest of the class. Observe and coach each set of actors. Encourage the other children to help you with the coaching. Give as many children as possible an opportunity to practice the four strategies.

 (Continued Next Page)

Four Ways to Say No ———— (Continued)

Lead a discussion. Following the dramatizations, get the children to talk about the strategies and what their use could mean. Ask these and other open-ended questions:

— *How did you feel when you said no?*
— *What was it like to say no and suggest something else to do?*
— *How did you feel when you said no and gave a reason?*
— *Which strategy was the easiest? Why?*
— *Which strategy was the hardest? Why?*
— *If you played Molly, which strategy do you think worked best?*
— *How did you feel when you walked away?*
— *Why is it hard to walk away from a friend?*
— *If you hurt your friend's feelings, or even lose your friend, by walking away, what can you do to feel better yourself?*
— *Why don't people take no for an answer?*

Conclude the activity. Thank the children for their good listening, acting, and thinking.

Practice Saying "No!"

Experience Sheet and Discussion

Relates to: Language Arts (reading, writing, listening, and speaking) K-3

Objectives: The children will:
— identify sources and effects of peer pressure.
— demonstrate appropriate behaviors in simulated peer pressure situations.

Note: This activity should be preceded by the role play and discussion activity, "Four Ways To Say No."

Time: approximately 30 minutes for readiness, work time, and discussion

Materials Needed: one copy of the experience sheet, "Practice Saying "No!," and a pencil for each child

Directions: **Introduce the activity.** Remind the children of the four strategies for responding to potentially harmful peer pressure. Ask them to describe the strategies to you. Clear up any misconceptions and, if necessary, review the four ways of saying no. Tell the children that they are going to have an opportunity to practice the strategies again, this time in writing.

Pass out the experience sheets and pencils. Go over the instructions with the children. Say to them: *Decide what you want Nick to say in the picture and write the words in his cartoon bubble. If you need help, ask a friend—or raise your hand and I'll help you.* Give the children about 10 minutes to finish the experience sheet.

Ask the children to get together in groups of four or five. Suggest that they show and tell one another what they wrote.

Lead a total group discussion. Ask these and/or other questions:
— *Which way did you decide to say no?*
— *Was it hard to write?*
— *Has anything like this ever happened to you?*
— *If you were Nick, would you be worried that Susan might not want to be your friend anymore? What could you do about that?*

Practice Saying "No!"

Susan and Nick are walking to school. Susan wants Nick to use his lunch money to buy sodas and candy at the corner store. Nick doesn't want to stop at the store. He wants to save his lunch money for pizza and milk at school.

Read what Susan says. What do you think Nick should say back? Write his words in the bubble. Pick one of the four ways to say no:

    1. Say no
    2. Say no and suggest something else to do.
    3. Say no and give a reason.
    4. Say no and leave.

Hey Nick, Let's use our lunch money to buy a soda and Fudgenuckle Bar. No one will ever even know . . . Come on let's do it!

It Was Hard, But I Said No

A Sharing Circle

Relates to: Language Arts (oral language) 4-6

Objectives: The children will demonstrate appropriate behaviors when peer pressure is contrary to their beliefs.

Directions: **Review the sharing circle rules as necessary.**

State the topic. Say to the children: *Has anyone ever asked you to do something that you knew was wrong or not good for you? Maybe the thing this person asked you to do sounded like fun, so it was hard to say no—but you did. Things like that happen to all of us, not just while we're growing up, but even as adults—so it's important to learn to say no. Today, let's talk about how we can do that. Our topic is, "It Was Hard, But I Said No."*

Think of a time when you really wanted to do something, but you knew you shouldn't, so you said no. Maybe a friend asked you to come over after school, but your mother wanted you to come straight home, so you said no. Or maybe someone asked you to trade your sandwich for a candy bar, but you knew that wouldn't be a good lunch, so you said no. Did anyone ever ask you to tell a lie so he or she wouldn't get into trouble? Or keep quiet about something? Or smoke a cigarette? Tell us about something like this that happed to you, but don't say who asked you to do it. Think about it for a moment or two, and raise your hand when you are ready to share. The topic is, "It Was Hard, But I Said No."

Involve the children in sharing.

Conduct a summary. After everyone who wants to speak has done so, encourage the children to talk about what they learned. Ask these and other questions to generate a discussion:
— *How did you feel when you said no?*
— *What did the other person do or say when you said no?*
— *Why is it hard to say no?*
— *How can we learn to say no to people who ask us to do things that are wrong or bad for us?*

Conclude the sharing circle.

Menu-for-a-Day

Experience Sheet and Discussion

Relates to: Health (nutrition) and Math, 4-6

Objectives:

The children will:
— describe how health may affect or be affected by stress.
— demonstrate knowledge of good health habits.

Time:

approximately 20 to 25 minutes

Materials Needed:

a pencil and one copy of the experience sheet, "Menu-for-a-Day" for each child

Directions:

Introduce the activity. Review the four basic food groups. Discuss the number of recommended servings from each group that children should eat each day for optimum health. Write these on the chalkboard along with *specific* examples of the kinds of food found in each group. Save the list for the children to refer to as they work.

Say to the children: *Do you know what a dietician is? A dietician is a person whose job it is to plan healthful meals, recipes, and menus for other people. Dieticians work in hospitals, food processing plants, laboratories and even hotels. They base many of their decisions on a knowledge of the four basic food groups. Today, you and a partner are going to be working as a team of dieticians. Your job is to plan tasty and healthful meals and snacks for one full day.*

Distribute the experience sheets. Have the children choose partners and allow sufficient time for them to complete their menus. Circulate and offer assistance, as necessary.

(Continued Next Page)

Lead a discussion. Have the children share their completed menus with the class, explaining why they chose various menu items. Ask these and other questions to stimulate a discussion:

— *Which is your favorite food group?*

— *Which food group do you like least? Why?*

— *Where does candy fit in the basic food groups? Why do you think that is?*

— *What do you think would happen (at school, at home) if you didn't get enough to eat?*

— *What might happen if you didn't get food from all the basic food groups?*

— *If you are hungry, can you concentrate on your school work?*

— *How does stress affect health, and what are some things you can do to relieve stress?*

Conclude the activity. Discuss with the children some of the benefits of good nutrition and the problems associated with poor nutrition. Compliment the children on their menu-planning skills.

Menu-for-a-Day

Make a menu for one day. Use the 4 food groups. Each time you choose a food that belongs to one of the food groups, put a check mark (√) next to the name of the group.

The 4 Food Groups	Number of servings each day
Fruits and vegetables	4
Breads and cereals	4
Milk and milk products	3-4
Meat, fish, poultry, eggs	2

Menu

Breakfast   **mid-morning snack**

Lunch   **mid-afternoon snack**

Dinner   **bedtime snack**

Human Pressure Machines

Creative Movement and Discussion

Relates to: Social Studies, Language Arts and Physical Education, 4-6

Objectives:	The children will identify sources and effects of peer pressure.
Time:	approximately 30 minutes
Materials Needed:	tumbling mats or a grassy outdoor space where groups of five to six children can move freely
Directions:	**Begin by discussing with the children the concept of negative peer pressure.** Say to the children: *When your friends or classmates, who are called your peers, try to persuade you to do, say, or believe something that you are against—that's peer pressure. They may bribe, persist, bug, or hassle you. They may include you, or exclude you from a group. For example, someone might say that you are not really a friend unless you let him or her copy the answers to the math homework.*
	Brainstorm other situations with the class and write them on the board. Explain that peer pressure is like a machine that keeps doing the same movements over and over until someone shuts it off.
	Divide the children into groups of five or six and ask them to create moving "human pressure machines." Suggest that they think of movements that will create pressure on each other and receive pressure from each other. For example, one person might lie on the mat or grass and move his or her feet to push on the shoulders of another person. The second person in turn might pull on the arms of a third person, and so on to create a chain of movements. Each member of the group becomes a different part of the machine by moving in a different way. Tell the children to create a way to "turn of" their machine.

(Continued Next Page)

Allow the children about ten minutes to create and rehearse their peer pressure machines. Circulate among the groups, encouraging them and offering suggestions to those who are having difficulty. Then invite each group to perform for the whole class.

Lead as summary discussion. Ask the children to compare their human pressure machines to how peer pressure works in real life. Ask these and other questions to spark a discussion:

— *How did it feel to be physically pressured in your machine?*
— *In what ways is peer pressure like the machine you created?*
— *Why do you think it is important to talk about and understand peer pressure?*
— *How is peer pressure a form of stress?*

Conclude the activity. Thank the children for their creative participation.

Resisting Peer Pressure

Assertiveness Practice

Relates to: **Social Studies and Language Arts (oral language) 4-6**

Objectives: The children will demonstrate appropriate behaviors when peer pressures are contrary to their beliefs.

Time: approximately 30 minutes

Directions: **Review the concept of negative peer pressure.** Ask the students to explain the concept in their own words. Try to arrive at a definition that includes these elements: *Peer pressure is when someone about your age tries to get you to do, say, or believe something that you don't want to do, say, or believe.*

Explain to the children: *One of the most powerful ways to resist peer pressure is to use an "I" message. When you use an "I" message, you are telling the other person how you feel, what you think, and what you want or don't want to do. Statements like this are called "I" messages because they often start with the word "I." Because they focus on how I feel, they make me feel stronger without putting down the other person. In fact, they frequently improve the situation. On the other hand, messages that start with "you" are often put-downs. They frequently make matters worse.*

Give some examples of "I" messages:

1. I feel upset when you want me to take something from home without my parents' permission. I would rather ask first.

2. I don't want to give you the answers to my math homework problems. I worked hard to figure them out myself.

3. I don't want to get into trouble for staying out after dark. I want to go home.

4. I don't want to smoke a cigarette. I don't like the bad things it can do to me.

 (Continued Next Page)

Resisting Peer Pressure

Compare them with corresponding "you" messages:

1. You bug me when you ask me to take something from home without permission. Take it from your house.

2. You're lazy! Do the math problems yourself!

3. You are always trying to get me into trouble. Stay outside in the dark by yourself.

4. You shouldn't smoke. It's bad for you.

Let the children add to your list of "I" messages. Write them on the chalkboard or butcher paper. Ask the children to think of corresponding "you" messages as well.

Conduct a practice session. After you have completed the list, ask the children to choose a partner with whom to practice. Have the partners take turns delivering first an "I" message and then the corresponding "you" message from the list. Finally, make up new situations and let the partners role play delivering "I" and "you" messages to each other. Ask some pairs to demonstrate in front of the class.

Summarize by asking the children how they felt when they received an "I" message as compared to a "you" message.

Conclude the activity. Thank the children for contributing their ideas. Ask them to practice "I" messages on the playground and at home.

Something I Do to Take Care of Myself

A Sharing Circle

Relates to: Language Arts (oral language) 4-6

Objectives: The children will demonstrate knowledge of good health habits.

Directions: **Review the sharing circle rules as necessary.**

State the topic. Say to the children: *I'm sure most of us like to feel healthy and have plenty of energy. In order to feel good, we need to take care of ourselves. Today's topic is "Something I Do to Take Care of Myself."*

There are many things we can do to take care of ourselves. The things you do might include going to bed early so you get plenty of sleep, or eating a healthy breakfast in the morning. Maybe you watch your favorite T.V. show because it makes you laugh and feel good. Or maybe you stay quiet and listen to soft music when you don't feel well. Whatever it is that you do for yourself, take a minute to think about it silently before we share. The topic is "Something I Do to Take Care of Myself."

Involve the children in sharing.

Conduct a summary. When every child in the circle has had a chance to speak, ask some questions to help the children summarize what they have learned:
— *Why is it helpful to talk about the ways in which we take care of ourselves?*
— *How do you feel about doing things that are good for you?*
— *What could happen if you didn't take care of yourself?*
— *What have you learned about staying healthy and stress-free?*

Conclude the sharing circle.

A Garden of Healthy Habits

Art and Discussion

Relates to: Health, Art, and Language Arts (writing and oral language) 4-6

Objectives:	The children will demonstrate knowledge of good health habits.
Time:	approximately 30 minutes
Materials Needed:	chalkboard or chart paper, chalk, magic markers or crayons, construction paper in many colors, glue, and scissors
Directions:	**Explain the activity to the children.** Tell them that you would like everyone to spend some time discussing good health habits. Begin by listing on the chalkboard or chart paper the good health habits mentioned in the sharing circle "Something I Do to Take Care of Myself." Then brainstorm additional good health habits and add them to the list. Solicit specific examples such as: "I floss my teeth daily," "I eat healthy foods," "I only take drugs that the doctor prescribes for me," "I laugh and tell jokes to feel good and reduce stress."

Make the flowers for the garden. Distribute the art materials. Tell the children that they are going to make flowers out of construction paper and decorate them with crayons or magic markers. Explain that each petal of their flower will symbolize one thing they do to take care of themselves.

Give the children the following directions, demonstrating each step of the process: *Cut out a circle for the center of the flower, and five to eight petals. Cut out a stem and some leaves, too. Write your name in the center of the flower. On each petal, print one of your own good health habits. Choose health habits from the list or think of new ones, but be sure they are habits you practice. After you have finished labeling your petals, glue the flower together.*

As the children work, talk with them about how they take responsibility for their wellness.

Create the garden. When the flowers have all "bloomed", place them in a row on a bulletin board or wall. Title them "A Garden of Healthy Habits."

Conclude the activity. Thank the children for their participation and tell them how pleased you are with the garden they have created.

LEARNING RESPONSIBILITY

Achieving success in our lives depends upon developing responsible behavior, including the ability to effectively listen to others, understand what is heard, keep agreements, and take initiative. The activities in this section allow the students to learn the skills necessary to develop this important attribute.

Someday, Said Mitchell

Relates to: Language Arts
(literature and oral language) K-3

Objectives: The children will identify personal behaviors required for success in school and family situations, as well as habits and behaviors that hinder success.

Note: This is the first of three activities in which children begin to identify both positive behaviors that lead to success at school and at home, and neglectful or destructive behaviors that lead to unhappiness and failure.

Time: approximately 20 minutes

Materials Needed: a copy of the storybook, *Someday, Said Mitchell,* written and illustrated by Barbara Williams, E. P. Dutton, New York, 1976

Directions: **Gather the children together.** Read the story to the children with enthusiasm and drama. Frequently invite their comments and ideas concerning what will happen next.

Lead a discussion. Use these questions and others to facilitate a discussion:
—*Did Mitchell love his mother and want to help her?*
—*How did Mitchell's mother like his promises about what he would do for her when he grew up?*
—*What did she want from Mitchell instead of promises?*
—*Did Mitchell's mother give you any ideas for what you could do to help out at home?*
—*What else could you do at home to be helpful?*
—*What are some unhelpful things children sometimes do at home—things they should stop doing or never do at all?*

Conclude the activity. Thank the children for their attention *and* for sharing their ideas with the group.

How I Help at School ——*A Sharing Circle*

Relates to: Language Arts (oral language) K-3

Objectives: The children will identify personal behaviors required for success in school and family situations, as well as habits and behaviors that hinder success.

Note: This sharing circle is the second of three activities that focus on effective behaviors, this time as they pertain to the school setting.

Directions: **Review the sharing circle rules as necessary.**

State the topic. In your own words, ask the children: *Do you remember what we talked about in our last sharing circle? (The children respond.) Yes! We told one another about times we felt unhappy. Everybody has feelings. Sometimes our feelings are nice and sometimes they aren't so nice. Today we are going to talk about things that we do here at school that other people usually like, things that make them feel happy. Our topic is, "How I Help at School."*

We've been talking lately about how we can be helpful at home. Now we are going to discuss how we can help out here at school. Think about it. What do you like to do here at school to help? Perhaps what you do helps some friends. Maybe you share things with them. Maybe you help me. Teachers always like it so much when the children are helpful. Or maybe you are helpful to yourself. You pay close attention and try to learn as much as you can because you know you are helping yourself when you do that. Tell us one way that you are helpful at school. Let's take a few moments to think it over before we start to share. The topic is, "How I Help at School." Raise your hand when you are ready.

Involve the children in sharing.

 (Continued Next Page)

How I Help at School —————— *(Continued)*

Conduct a summary. Here are three questions to ask the children. Use them to help generate a discussion:

—*What are some of the things we heard about that are helpful to do at school?*

—*Can you think of any other helpful things children can do at school?*

—*Can you think of any things children shouldn't do at school because they are <u>not</u> helpful?"*

In the course of the discussion, generate as many ideas as possible about helpful behaviors. Talk about how everyone gains when people help one another. Assist the children to recognize that there are unhelpful behaviors that deserve attention too, behaviors which benefit no one and should be avoided.

Conclude the sharing circle.

When I Help at School —— *An Art Activity*

Relates to: Art and Language Arts
(oral language) K-3

Objectives: The children will identify personal behaviors required for success in school and family situations, as well as habits and behaviors that can hinder success.

Note: This is the third of three related activities about helping. It underscores the importance of positive behaviors, particularly in the school setting.

Time: approximately 25 to 30 minutes

Materials Needed: sturdy art paper, water with dissolved sugar (one quarter cup sugar to one cup water), colored chalk, and fixative

Directions: **Remind the children about the sharing circle.** In your own words, ask, *Who remembers what we talked about in our sharing circle?* (The children respond.) *Good for you! We told each other about how we help at school. Sometimes we do things that help our friends; sometimes we do things to help the teacher; and sometimes we do things that help ourselves. Now let's make a picture of something we do at school that is helpful. Be sure to put yourself in your picture. Show yourself doing the helpful thing you told us about in the sharing circle.*

Demonstrate: Tell the children, *We're going draw with chalk on paper that is wet with sugar water. Our drawings could get pretty sticky and messy, so we will need to help one another as we do this. Let me show you how.*

With a wide brush, apply the sugar water to your sheet of paper. Then, as the children watch, use the chalk to draw a picture of yourself doing the helpful action that you described in the sharing circle. Keep the picture "primitive," but fill up the entire sheet of paper with figures and objects. Mention to the children that you are making everything very big, so that the picture can be seen easily.

 (Continued Next Page)

Get the children started. Apply sugar water to each child's sheet of paper, supply chalk, and help the children remember the helpful actions that they talked about in the sharing circle.

As the children work on their pictures, circulate and create conversation. Ask them to tell you about their pictures. Be sure to compliment their efforts.

Conclude the activity. When the children have finished their drawings, you may wish to display them on a bulletin board, or wall. Place a header above them that says, "How We Help at School." The next day, enjoy viewing the display together.

How Members of My Family Support and Help One Another

A Sharing Circle

Relates to: Language Arts (oral language) K-3

Objectives: The children will describe the interdependence of the family unit in terms of working together and sharing responsibilities.

Directions: **Review the sharing circle rules as necessary.**

State the topic. Say to the children: *Our topic today is, "How the Members of My Family Support and Help One Another." A characteristic of families that we sometimes take for granted is that family members are constantly helping one another. We do many big and small things for each other every day. Think of an example of how one member of your family helps another. Maybe your dad helps your brother or sister with homework, or your mom drives your grandmother to her appointments with the doctor. Possibly your older brother or sister occasionally plays your favorite game with you or helps you put together a tough puzzle. Did your parents ever help someone in the family who needed money for an emergency? Who do members of your family talk to when they have a problem? Take a few moments to think about it. When you have thought of something to share, raise your hand to show that you are ready. The topic is, "How the Members of My Family Support and Help One Another."*

Involve the children in sharing.

Conduct a summary. After all of the children have had an opportunity to share, encourage them to talk about what they learned in the circle. Ask these and other open-ended questions to help generate a discussion:
— *Why do family members help one another?*
— *What can happen to a family member who is seldom willing to help others?*
— *Is it okay to ask for help when you need it? Why or why not?*

Conclude the sharing circle.

I Kept Trying Until I Learned It

Relates to: Language Arts (oral language) K-3

Objectives: The children will demonstrate an understanding of the importance of practice, effort, and learning.

Note: This is the first of two sequential activities focusing on learning tasks. It allows the children to talk about the process of learning a new task, and prepares them for the learning center project, "The 'Do It Myself' Center."

Directions: **Review the sharing circle rules as necessary.**

State the topic. *Today we are going to talk about learning. Some things are easy to learn and we learn them quickly; however, most of the time, it takes practice to learn something new. We may have to try many times before we do it right. Our topic today is, "I Kept Trying Until I Learned It."*

Can you think of a time when you tried to learn something and it didn't come easily to you? Maybe you were trying to learn how to tie your shoes or comb your hair. Perhaps you were trying very hard to color within the lines, or tell time. Whatever it was, it was hard for you and you didn't learn it right away. But you didn't give up either—you kept trying. You worked at it. Think about it for a moment, and when you are ready to share, raise your hand. The topic is, " I Kept Trying Until I Learned It."

Involve the children in sharing.

(Continued Next Page)

Conduct a summary. When every child who wants to share has done so, involve the children in a discussion of what they heard. Here are some questions to ask them:

— *Did anyone else have a hard time learning some of the things that were shared? Which ones?*

— *How did you feel when you were trying, but couldn't seem to learn the thing?*

— *How did you feel when you finally learned how to do it?*

— *Did anyone feel like giving up?*

— *What would have happened if you had given up?*

Point out that everyone is always learning, and that it is important to keep trying even when it seems we might not be able to accomplish all that we would like to. Some people learn things faster and more easily than others, but eventually we all learn them, providing we don't give up.

Conclude the sharing circle.

The "Do It Myself!" Center ───────

─────────────── *A Learning Center Project*

Relates to: Language Arts (reading and oral language) and Motor Skills Development, K-3

Objectives: The children will demonstrate an understanding of the importance of practice, effort, and learning.

Note: This is the second of two sequential activities that focus on learning tasks. It involves the children working independently to accomplish a variety of tasks. In conjunction with the learning center, conduct the sharing circle, "I Kept Trying Until I Learned It."

Time: approximately 10 to 15 minutes per visit to the learning center

Materials Needed: at least one complete set of learning-task cards (described below), and a box of props to go with them (for example, a shoe, zipper, shirt with buttons, primary-level writing paper and pencils, etc.); instruction chart, and work table or other appropriate furnishings

Directions: **Create a center where the children can practice basic tasks and monitor their own progress.** Develop one or more sets of cards (5-inch by 8-inch cards work nicely) with pictures showing specific tasks that you want the children to master. For example: Zip a zipper, tie a shoe, button a shirt, write your name, etc.

Prepare three envelopes with the labels, "By Myself," "With Help," and "Soon."

On 8 1/2-inch by 11-inch paper, make a simple chart on which the children can keep track of their own progress. With marking pens, draw a symbol for each task down the left side of the master chart (shoe, zipper, etc.) Make three columns on the chart, using headings identical to those on the three envelopes. Make a copy of the chart for each child who will be using the center and label it with the child's name. Place the charts in a folder or box at the center.

 (Continued Next Page)

The "Do It Myself!" Center —— (Continued)

Walk the children through the use of the center. Say to them: *When you come to the center, take a set of cards. Go through the cards one at a time. Look in the box or on the table and find the objects that go with the card. Then practice the task shown on the card. For example, if the card tells you to write your name, get a piece of paper and a crayon from the table and practice writing your name. If the card tells you to tie a shoe, get the shoe out of the box and practice tying it. If you need help, ask a friend to help you.*

When you have finished practicing the task, put the card in one of the envelopes. If you did the task by yourself, put it in the "I Did It By Myself" envelope. If you did it with help, put it in the "With Help" envelope. If you still need to practice, put it in the "Soon" envelope.

When you have finished going through the cards, find the sheet with your name on it and put a check in one of the columns next to each thing you did.

Demonstrate the use of the progress charts and go over the words that the children will have to recognize. In addition to the walk-through and demonstration, repeat the instructions in chart form and place the chart at the center. Use symbols in place of words wherever possible.

Talk to the children periodically about their progress. Here are some questions you can ask:
— *How many of you can _____ all by yourself?*
— *Why is it important to practice?*
— *What are you working on now?*

Celebrate the progress of individuals, and encourage the efforts of all of the children.

Indoor Garden

Growing Alfalfa Sprouts

Relates to: Science, Health, and Math, K-3

Objectives: The children will describe the importance of working together to accomplish a task.

Time: approximately 5 to 10 minutes a day for four days

Materials Needed: one set of the following equipment for each group of three students: alfalfa seeds, wide-mouthed jar, cheesecloth or nylon netting, strong rubber band, tablespoon, and label

Directions: **Talk to the children about the fundamentals of growing plants.** Ask them:
—*Do you have gardens or plants at home?*
—*What do you think you would need in order to grow vegetables, flowers, and house plants?*
—*Have you ever grown a plant without dirt or soil?*

Some of the children may have sprouted an avocado seed or other seedlings in water. Explain that this is possible because when it sprouts, a plant gets most of the food it needs directly from its own seed. Seeds don't need to be in soil to start growing. Tell the children that they are going to find out for themselves by growing a nutritious crop—alfalfa sprouts—without soil.

Explain to the children in simple terms that growing plants without soil is one of the ways that food production can be increased in countries where good soil and natural water supplies are severely limited. Tell them that sprouted beans and seeds (such as they are going to grow) are easy, bountiful food crops to cultivate and could help feed people throughout the world who are not getting enough to eat. On chalk board or chart paper, draw a simple diagram or pictorial equation showing one pound of alfalfa seeds equaling (or yielding) eight pounds of sprouts.

     (Continued Next Page)

Indoor Garden ———————— (Continued)

Divide the children into groups of three. Name or number the groups, and list the names (or numbers) on a single chart. Give each group a set of supplies. Guide the groups through the following steps, providing assistance as needed. Have the children put a check mark on the chart each time their group completes step 4 over the four day period. (**Note:** These directions will also grow radish or clover sprouts.)

1. Scoop two or three tablespoons of alfalfa seeds into a one-quart, wide-mouthed jar. Cover the mouth with cheesecloth or nylon netting and secure with a strong rubber band. (Use masking tape or a gummed label to identify each group's jar.)

2. Pour tap water into the jar, swish it about to rinse the seeds clean, and pour off the water. Add enough tap water to generously cover the seeds and let them soak.

3. Soak the seeds for three to six hours, then drain the water from the jar. Place the jar on its side, at an angle, to provide growing space for the sprouts and to allow any extra water to drain off. Keep the jar out of direct sunlight.

4. Two or three times daily, rinse the seeds, filling the jar with cool tap water through the netted lid. Drain well and place the jar back on its side. The sprouts are ready for harvest when the hulls can easily be slipped off. Usually this point is reached in about four days. If desired, the sprouts can be swirled in a pan of cool water to remove the hulls, which will float to the top and can be skimmed off.

5. To green the sprouts, move them to a sunny windowsill, then transfer them to a glass jar and refrigerate. They are ready to eat!

 (Continued Next Page)

Indoor Garden ———————————— (Continued)

Sample the sprouts together. Use them to garnish little sandwiches or as a salad ingredient—or both. Talk to the children about the experience of growing and eating the sprouts. Ask these and other questions to generate a discussion:

— *How do you like the sprouts?*

— *What did you like most about growing the sprouts?*

— *How did your group work together?*

— *How did you share the different jobs involved?*

— *Were you surprised that the sprouts grew so fast?*

— *I think that their fast growth would make sprouts a good food to grow in countries where lots of people are hungry. What do you think?*

— *Do you think you could grow sprouts at home?*

Conclude the activity. Thank the children for their cooperation and productivity.

We Worked Together to Get It Done —

A Sharing Circle

Relates to: Language Arts (oral language) K-3

Objectives: The children will describe the importance of cooperation in accomplishing a task.

Directions: **Review the sharing circle rules as necessary.**

State the topic. *Our topic for today is, "We Worked Together to Get It Done." Many times we do things all by ourselves, but sometimes it is necessary or more fun to do things with other people. Think of a time when you did something with others. Perhaps you and a friend, or you and your family, worked together to finish something—like a Halloween costume, or a holiday dinner. Maybe you and your Mom did the dishes together, or you and a friend put together a puzzle. Have you and a brother or sister ever worked together to make cookies, or build a sand castle? Think about it for a minute or two, and when you are ready to share, please raise your hand. The topic is, "We Worked Together to Get It Done."*

Involve the children in sharing.

Conduct a summary. Ask these and other questions to stimulate a free-flowing discussion:
— *Do you think it is easier to get the job done with other people helping?*
— *How did you decide who was going to do what?*
— *If you were going to do the same job again, would you do the part of the job that you did this time, or would you do a different part of the job? Which part?*

Conclude the sharing circle.

Princess Furball Earns Her Wishes —

Listening and Discussion

Relates to: **Language Arts (listening and oral language) K-3**

Objectives:
The children will:
—describe relationships among ability, effort, and achievement.
—demonstrate an understanding of the importance of practice, effort, and learning.

Time:
approximately 30 minutes

Materials Needed:
a copy of *Princess Furball* by Charlotte Huck, illustrated by Anita Lobel, New York, Greenwillow Books, 1989

Directions:
Gather the children together and read *Princess Furball* to them. It is a variant of the Cinderella story in which a princess runs away from a greedy father who tries to marry her to an ugly ogre in exchange for fifty wagons of silver. To survive, she uses the skills that a nurse and a cook taught her and hides her identify from a young king to give him time to fall in love with her. Read the story twice, as this version may not be familiar to the children.

Lead a discussion, using the following questions as a guide:
—*What kinds of things did Princess Furball learn to do when she was a little girl?*
—*How did the skills that Furball learned while she was young help her escape from her greedy father? ...survive in another kingdom? ...win the love of the young king?*
—*What makes this story different from the Cinderella story that we have read before?*
—*Which princess do you like better, Cinderella or Furball? Why?*
—*What are some things you are learning in school today that will help you when you are grown up? How will they help you?*
(List these on the board.)

(Continued Next Page)

Conclude the activity. Ask the children to think about how, even though we may have the ability to do something (like Furball's ability to make good soup), we must try our hardest and learn as much as we can.

Extension:

• Invite the children to illustrate one thing that they are learning in school. Below the picture, have them (or help them) write a sentence or two describing how it will help them in the future.

• Read the fairy tale *The Enchanted Book* by Janina Porazinska, translated by Bozena Smith, illustrated by Jan Brett, San Diego, Harcourt Brace, Jovanovich, 1987. This is a re-telling of a traditional Polish tale in which the miller's youngest daughter succeeds in outwitting an evil sorcerer by using her ability to read.

Making a Butter Churn

Relates to: Language Arts and Social Studies (history and folklore) K-3

Objectives: The children will describe the importance of cooperation among workers in accomplishing a task.

Note: This is the first of two sequential activities addressing the concept of working together. It should be followed by the group enterprise, "Making Butter."

Time: approximately 15 minutes to present facts and history, 10 to 15 minutes to construct butter churns, and 5 to 10 minutes for discussion

Materials Needed: for <u>each</u> butter churn: a coffee can, glass jar, or tall wide-mouth container with a snap-fit plastic lid; eight 1-inch dowels; one 12-inch dowel; and one wheel with holes into which to fit the dowels (Tinkertoy parts work well for the dowels and wheel)

Directions: **Tell the children something about the history of butter-making.** Select from the information that follows, offering the children as much or as little as you deem appropriate. List words or terms that you would like the children to learn on chart paper or poster board. Illustrate them with simple drawings or pictures cut from magazines.

Butter has been made for thousands of years by churning the fat from milk. Not only was butter a tasty spread for bread, it was also used to fry foods and to make pastries. The Greeks and Romans even used it as a remedy for burns and skin injuries.

Butter was not only made from cow's milk, but also from the milk of goats, sheep, and buffaloes. Early butter-making technique consisted of churning the milk of goats and sheep in a leather-skin bag that was swung back and forth to agitate the milk and separate the fat. Later, milk or cream was placed in churns that were rocked, shaken, or swung to separate the fat.

In early America, butter was a luxury. The families that had milk cows made butter and traded with their neighbors for other simple items. When milking-cows became more plentiful along with the supply of milk, many more families had butter churns and made their own butter.

Two types of churns were commonly used. The first was a tall wooden

(Continued Next Page)

bucket with a long dasher (wooden stick with a round blunt end like that of a wooden potato masher) that required a lot of arm-pumping. The dasher was plunged up and down in the churn until butter was formed. The second was the rocking churn that was also a wooden box with a tight-fitting cover that sat on rockers so the feet could do the "rocking," leaving the hands free to work on a different task.

In early America, pails of milk were left to sit until the milk began to sour and the cream could then be skimmed from the top and placed in the butter churn. Since it was an easy but long, tiring job to continuously move the dasher, the job was frequently given to children. To make the job more pleasant, the children chanted butter-churning rhymes in time to the up-down rhythms of the dasher motions. One example:

> *Churn better churn*
> *Churn butter churn*
> *Mary smiling with her plate*
> *Waiting for a butter cake*
> *Churn butter churn*

After a great deal of churning, the cream would begin to bubble and foam. Following more beating, the cream slowly turned into floating lumps or curds of butter.

When no more butter lumps would "come," the butter was scooped out of the churn. The white liquid that remained was the buttermilk. The buttermilk was drained from the churn and the butter washed in cold water, drained, and salted. This butter was stirred to thoroughly mix the salt and obtain the right texture. Salt was added both for flavor and as a preservative. (The buttermilk was often given to the children as a reward for their hard work of churning the cream into butter.)

The natural color of butter varies from almost white to deep gold. The color depends on the kind of cows from which the milk is obtained, and the feed eaten by the cows. When cows feed in pastures, their milk has a deeper color than when they receive dry feed in the barns. Butter is often colored with food dyes because people like to have butter be a uniform golden color.

In early America, wooden butter molds with traditional designs of eagles, wheat, or thistle carved into them made raised designs when stamped onto butter squares. Many butter makers were proud of their products so their butter mold design became their trademark.

The butter recipe has not changed, but modern machinery at the creamery now makes the butter. The United States is a leading producer of butter, particularly in the states of Wisconsin, Minnesota, and Iowa.

Additional facts: It takes the cream from approximately ten quarts of milk to equal one pound of butter. The food value of butter is 80% butterfat, 16% water, 3% salt, and 1% curd of milk. Since butter contains so much fat, it is one of the richest food sources of heat and energy. Butter contains large quantities of vitamin A. One pound of butter contains about 3,200 calories.

(Continued Next Page)

Making a Butter Churn —————— (Continued)

Have the children construct the butter churns. Form groups of five to six children. (These will be the same groups that will work together to make the butter in the next activity.) Give each group a set of materials. Guide the groups through the following steps, suggesting that the children take turns performing the various tasks involved, and offering assistance as needed:

1. Use the coffee can or other container as the bucket of the butter churn.
2. To form the dasher, insert one end of the 12-inch piece of wood dowel into the center of the wheel.
3. Insert the eight 1-inch dowels into the holes of the wheel.
4. In the center of the plastic lid, cut or punch a hole large enough for the dowel handle to slide through easily.
5. Place the dasher in the can, slip the plastic lid over the dowel handle, and snap the lid into place on the container. The handle should stick out far enough to be grasped easily.

Conclude the activity. Collect the butter churns and thank the children for cooperating to make them. Announce when the butter-making activity will take place.

Making Butter ——— *A Group Enterprise*

Relates to: Social Studies (history and folklore) and Health (nutrition) K-3

Objectives: The children will describe the importance of cooperation in accomplishing a task.

Note: This is the second of two sequential activities addressing the concept of working together. It follows the tool-making project, "Making a Butter Churn."

Time: approximately 60 to 75 minutes

Materials Needed: butter churns (from the previous activity), heavy whipping cream (approximately 1/2 pint per churn), salt, yellow food coloring, bread, plastic knives, bowls and stir spoons (one per group), containers in which to save the buttermilk (optional), small cookie cutters (optional), and toothpicks

Directions: **Preparation:** Let the cream stand at room temperature for several hours.

Introduce the activity. Remind the children of the history of butter-making. Ask them to share what they can remember and fill in any important points they have forgotten. Explain to the children that they will be working in the same groups that made the butter churns in the previous activity. Say to them: *Now you will use your churn to make butter. Since it takes a long time to churn cream into butter, you can take turns doing the work.*

Have the children form their small groups and redistribute the butter churns. Pour enough room-temperature cream into each churn to make it about half full.

Lead the children through the butter-making enterprise. Tell them to place their lid tightly on the churn and begin beating the dasher up and down with a steady rhythm. Lead the children in chanting "Churn Butter Churn" (see previous activity) or some other rhyme.

(Continued Next Page)

Have the children take turns beating the dasher with each group continuing to offer encouragement and/or chanting rhymes to make the churning go more easily. After twenty or thirty minutes, the butter should "come" in the form of lumps that float on the top of the liquid and stick to the dasher. Sometimes the cream will turn to whipped cream before the butter curds form—if this happens, just continue churning with the dasher.

When no more curds form, have the children remove the lid and scoop out the butter curds. Collect and save the buttermilk (optional). The butter will be quite soft and mushy. Put the curds in bowls and rinse them under cold running water to remove any milk left in the butter.

Cool the butter in the refrigerator. In about an hour, the butter balls will be firm enough to mold together. Have the children stir a little salt and a few drops of yellow food coloring into the butter, to give it the familiar taste and look of store-bought butter.

Show the children how to shape the butter into balls, sticks, or pats. Or let them cut it into shapes using small cookie cutters. Suggest that the children carve designs on the butter using the point of a toothpick.

Give each group some bread and one or more plastic knives. Let them spread some of their butter on the bread, serving and enjoying the results of their labor.

Lead a discussion. While enjoying this special snack, generate a conversation focusing on the process of butter-making. Ask such questions as:
—*Does anyone think that he or she could make butter alone?*
—*What would be hard about making butter by yourself?*
—*Were you glad that there were others in your group, so that you could share the churning?*
—*What would have happened if some people hadn't done their share of churning?*
—*Could you have made your butter churn alone?*
—*Which was easier to make, the butter churn or the butter?*
—*Why is it important for people to work together on some jobs?*

Conclude the activity. Thank the children for their cooperation, hard work, and tasty results.

Who Helps In Your Family?

Experience Sheet, Discussion, and Drawing

Relates to: Language Arts (reading and writing) and Art, K-3

Objectives: The children will describe the interdependence of the family unit in terms of working together and sharing responsibilities.

Time: approximately 15 minutes to complete the experience sheet and15 minutes for discussion

Materials Needed: one copy of the Experience Sheet, "Who Helps in Your Family?" for each child; drawing paper and crayons, colored pencils, or marking pens

Directions: **Distribute the experience sheet, "Who Helps in Your Family?"** Give the children a few minutes to complete it. Pair readers with non-readers, or have older children or adult volunteers assist non-readers.

Alternative: Proceed with the discussion outlined below, and *then* have the children complete the experience sheets.

Lead a discussion. Talk about the way family members work together. Ask questions about the first picture on the experience sheet. For example:
— *What is this family doing?*
— *What is the child doing?*
— *What are the mother and father doing?*
— *Who shops in your family?*
— *Do you sometimes help with shopping? What do you do to help?*

Look at the second picture together and ask these and other questions:
—*What is this family doing?*
—*What is the father doing?*
—*What are the children doing?*
—*What do you do to help keep your house clean?*

    (Continued Next Page)

Who Helps In Your Family? — *(Continued)*

Look at the third picture together and ask these and other questions:
— *What is this family doing?*
— *Who is using the computer?*
— *Have you ever used a computer? What did you use it for?*
— *Why is it important for families to learn together?*

Ask the children to talk about other things their families do together:
— *Does your family play games together? Which ones?*
— *Does your family have a yard? Who helps clean the yard?*
— *Does someone help you by driving you to school?*
— *What do you do to help other members of your family?*

Ask each child to draw a picture showing one of the things his or her family does together. Distribute the drawing materials. Then explain to the children: *You can draw a picture of your family shopping together, cleaning together, playing together, eating together, learning together, or doing some other thing together. It doesn't matter how big or how small your family is. Maybe you live with just your mother, or your grandparent. That's a fine family, and we want to see what you do together.*

Add captions to the finished pictures. Display them around the room. Let the children take turns showing their picture and talking about the activity they do with their family. Thank the children for their efforts.

Who Helps In Your Family?

Cleaning Together

Shopping Together

Learning Together

87

Who Helps In Your Family?

Who Helps In Your Family?

My _____ helps me read.

My _____ shops.

I help my _____ cook.

I help my _____ work.

mother	father	sister
aunt	cousin	grandfather
brother	grandmother	friend

88

Pinocchio's Advice ———————

———— *Listening, Discussion, and Letter-Writing*

Relates to: Language Arts (listening, speaking, and writing) K-3

Objectives: The children will describe what one can learn from making mistakes.

Time: three to four sessions, approximately 20 minutes each

Materials Needed: any version of the book, *Pinocchio*, by Carlo Collodi (such as the one translated and adapted by Mariana Mayer, illustrated by Gerald McDermott, New York, Four Winds Press, 1981); paper and pencils for all students

Directions: **Introduce the activity.** Inform the children that they are going to hear the story of a wooden puppet who came to life, but who made a few mistakes and had to pay the consequences. Read *Pinocchio* to the children. Depending on the version, it will take two or three 20-minute sessions.

After you have read the story, conduct a discussion of the central theme of the story: learning from mistakes. Use thought-provoking questions such as the ones below:
— *What were some of the "mistakes" that Pinocchio made?*
— *What were the consequences (results) of Pinocchio's behavior?*
— *How did Pinocchio's friends feel about his behavior?*
— *How do we feel when someone close to us is behaving selfishly?*
— *How did Pinocchio learn from his mistakes?*
— *Why is it important to think of other people as well as ourselves?*

Optional: Have the children divide into pairs or small groups to discuss the questions before sharing with the whole class. More children can participate in this way.

          (Continued Next Page)

After the discussion, ask the children to pretend that they are Pinocchio and write a letter of advice to another child. Show the children correct friendly-letter form on the board, or give them a template on which to write the letter. Invite them to close their eyes and pretend that they are Pinocchio, and have just become human after making several mistakes and paying the consequences. Ask them: *What would you tell your friend about yourself? What adventures would you describe? What advice would you give to your friend after you learned from your mistakes?*

Allow the children to make a rough drafts of their letter. Then divide the children into response groups, and ask them to read their rough drafts aloud and receive feedback from one another. Within each group, assign every member an editing job: Capitals Editor, Complete-Sentence Editor, Spelling Editor, Punctuation Editor (or divide the latter into periods, question marks and commas). Then direct the children to pass their letters around the group for each editor to check.

Provide good paper for final drafts of the letters. Post the letters on the bulletin board.

Conclude the activity. Acknowledge the children for being able to describe how someone learned from making mistakes, for writing the letters, and for working hard as editors.

Alternative for non-readers: Incorporate the suggestions and ideas of the children in a single letter that you write on the board. Keep the letter very simple. Read the completed letter to the children; read it a second time while the children follow along.

How My Mistake Helped Me Learn

Relates to: Language Arts (oral language) K-3

Objectives: The children will describe what one can learn from making mistakes.

Note: This sharing circle can precede or follow the "Pinocchio's Advice" letter-writing activity.

Directions: **Review the sharing circle rules as necessary.**

State the topic. Say to the children: *Often, when we make mistakes, we learn from them. Today's topic is, "How My Mistake Helped Me Learn."*

Have you ever pressed too hard on a new crayon and had the point break? After one or two broken points, you learned not to press so hard. That is an example of learning from a mistake. Mistakes are not so bad, if we learn from them. Perhaps when you were young, you started to run into the street. When your Dad or Mom or sitter saw you, he or she probably ran to get you and scolded you. Soon you learned that if you ran into the street, you would be scolded or punished. So you didn't do that anymore. Now that you are older, you know that learning not to run into the street may have saved your life. That is an example of learning from a mistake. Have you ever been late for school or a party because you were fooling around, and then missed out on something fun or important? You may have learned from that mistake. When you first learned to write, you probably made letters wrong. When someone showed you how to do it right, you learned from your mistake. Close your eyes for a moment and think of how a mistake helped you learn. Look up when you have thought of an example, and I'll know you are ready to talk and listen. The topic is, "How My Mistake Helped Me Learn."

(Continued Next Page)

How My Mistake Helped Me Learn —

(Continued)

Involve the children in sharing.

Conduct a summary. Ask open-ended questions like those below to help the children summarize what they have learned:
— *How is it helpful to make mistakes?*
— *How does it help to hear about the mistakes of other people?*
— *How do you feel after you have learned from a mistake?*
— *How do you think that learning from mistakes will help you in a job when you are older?*

Conclude the sharing circle.

Three-Step Plan for Success

Improving on a Weakness

Relates to: Language Arts (oral language and writing) 4-6

Objectives: The children will identify personal strengths and weaknesses in academic areas.

Time: approximately 30 minutes

Materials Needed: one copy of the experience sheet, "Three-Step Plan for Success," for each child; pencils and writing paper

Directions: Distribute the pencils and paper. Have the students write the heading, **"Things I Am Good At in School,"** at the top of their paper. Ask them to list three *specific* things under this heading. Suggest that they avoid naming general subjects. Explain: *Rather than simply saying that you are good at math and writing, for example, you might say that you are very good at recalling the multiplication tables and writing poems. Or you might say that you are good at conducting science experiments, naming the characteristics of mammals, estimating, counting money, giving oral reports, or reading mysteries.*

Below the first list, have the children write a second heading, **"Things I Need to Improve On in School."** Again, suggest that they list three specific items.

Distribute the experience sheets. Tell the children that you want them to write an "action plan" for one of the items on their improvement list. Have them pick an item, and write in the name of the item to complete the heading, **"My Plan for Improving in_____ "**

Step 1: Have the children choose partners. Explain that you want them to brainstorm specific ways that each of them can obtain help in his or her area of improvement. Say to them: *If you need to work on punctuation, maybe you can ask a student who is good at punctuation to work with you twice a week during recess. If you need to improve your spelling, maybe you can ask a parent or*

 (Continued Next Page)

older brother or sister to quiz you at home. Write down all the alternatives you come up with under the subheading, "How I Can Get Help."

Step 2: Point out that to improve their skill, the children will have to practice. Instruct the partners to again brainstorm alternatives and list them under the subheading, "Where and When I Will Practice My New Skill."

Step 3: Finally, ask the children to list the names of people to whom they might demonstrate their improved skill under the subheading, "To Whom I Will Show Off My New Skill."

When the three-step action plans are complete, ask volunteers to share their plans with the class. Pause at each step of a given action plan and invite the group to make additional suggestions. In this way, the children will be sure to have several alternatives to choose from. Even those who prefer not to share can benefit from listening to suggestions given to others, and will obtain new ideas for their own plans.

Challenge the children to put their improvement plans into action and report in a week on any progress made or obstacles encountered.

Lead a discussion. Encourage the children to talk about what they learned from the activity. Ask these and other open-ended questions:
—*How do you feel when you perform well in an area of study at school?*
—*How do you feel about improving in an area of weakness?*
—*How do you feel about getting help?*
—*Why is it important to make a plan of action when we want to improve in an area that is difficult?*

Conclude the activity. Thank the students for making an effort to improve in an area of difficulty. Acknowledge them for helping one another.

Three-Step Plan for Success

My Plan for Improving in _____

_____

How I Can Get Help:

_____

_____

_____

_____

_____

Where and When I Will Practice My New Skill:

_____

_____

_____

_____

_____

To Whom I Will Show Off My New Skill:

_____

_____

_____

_____

Creatures of Habit ———————

———————————— *A Group Discussion*

Relates to: Language Arts (oral language) 4-6

Objectives: | The children will identify personal behaviors required for success in school and family situations and habits and behaviors that hinder progress.

Note: This is the first in a series of five activities having to do with habits.

Time: | approximately 10 minutes

Directions: | **Introduce the activity.** Ask the children to join you for an important discussion. Explain to them that, throughout the next few activities, you will be talking about different kinds of habits and behaviors—some that help people, and some that hurt people.

Write the word *habit* on the chalkboard. Define it. Say to the children: *A habit is a behavior that is repeated over and over. Eventually the behavior is done very regularly and/or easily. Have you heard the expression, "creatures of habit?" It refers to the fact that people—and perhaps animals—seem to like to develop habits. We have lots of them.*

Let's think of some examples of creatures we know who have habits, both good and bad. Why not start with dogs? Do you have or know a dog who has a habit? Some of the habits of dogs are pretty funny.

Lead a brainstorming session. Call on several children. Ask them to tell the group about the habitual behaviors of dogs they know; write the names of the dogs and a word or two about each dog's habit on the chalkboard, under the heading "Dogs." Expect expressions of amusement on the part of the children as this process unfolds.

Next, invite the children to name the habitual behaviors of another animal, such as cats. Again, make an abbreviated list of their statements, this time under the heading, "Cats."

 (Continued Next Page)

Then, write the heading, "Humans," on the chalkboard. Ask the children to name some habits that humans have (but not to name the humans who have them). Record abbreviated descriptions of these habits.

Write the following terms and definitions on the chalkboard:
    Adaptive behavior = makes one *more* "fit" for the situation/surroundings
    Maladaptive behavior = makes one *less* fit for the situation/surroundings
    Neutral behavior = has no affect on one's fit for the situation/surroundings

Discuss the three terms. Tell the children you that scientists use these terms and that you believe they (the children) are ready to use them too.

Label the animal and human behaviors. Go back and look at the charts. Discuss each habit and decide if the behavior is adaptive, maladaptive or neutral. When there is disagreement, allow the children to vote. Write the letter "A," "M," or "N" next to each habit.

Conclude the activity: When the labeling has been completed, thank the children for their participation and contributions. Remind them that they will have other opportunities to discuss habits and behaviors during the next few activities.

A Good Habit I Plan to Keep

A Sharing Circle

Relates to: Language Arts (oral language) 4-6

Objectives: The children will identify personal behaviors required for success in school and family situations, and habits and behaviors that hinder progress.

Directions: **Review the sharing circle rules as necessary.**

State the topic. In your own words, ask the children: *In this sharing circle, we're going to talk more about habits and behaviors—this time our own. The topic is, "A Good Habit I Plan to Keep."*

Most of us have both kinds of habits—helpful and not-so-helpful. In this session, we're going to talk about our good ones. Think of a good habit you have, like always greeting people when you see them, or saying thank you when someone does something for you. Maybe you make a habit of feeding your pet every morning, or helping at home in the kitchen every evening. Perhaps the habit that comes to your mind is a health habit, like brushing your teeth regularly, eating food that's good for you, or getting lots of exercise. Take a few moments to think about it. When you are ready to share, raise your hand. The topic is, "A Good Habit I Plan to Keep."

Involve the children in sharing.

Conduct a summary. Ask several open-ended questions to help generate a discussion of what was learned in the circle.
— *How does having a good habit cause you to feel about yourself?*
— *What good habits did you hear about that you'd like to develop?*
— *What's the difference between an adaptive habit and a maladaptive habit?*
— *How would you go about replacing a maladaptive habit with an adaptive habit?*

Conclude the sharing circle.

Habits On Display

Relates to: Art and Language Arts (reading and oral language) 4-6

Objectives: The children will:
— identify personal behaviors required for success in school and family situations and habits and behaviors that hinder progress.
— demonstrate positive attitudes about self.

Time: approximately 35 to 45 minutes for preparation, drawing, and writing; and 20 to 30 minutes for viewing and reading

Materials Needed: sturdy art paper in pastel colors, at least 8 1/2 inches by 11 inches in size; and crayons or colored pencils

Directions: **Introduce the activity.** Remind the children of the previous sharing circle, "A Good Habit I Plan to Keep." Tell them that you would enjoy seeing illustrations of the things they shared.
Explain: *Draw a picture of yourself doing the thing you told us about when you described your good habit. As you work on your picture, discuss your drawing with the person sitting next to you. When the art work is finished, your partner will write a caption for your drawing, explaining what you are doing in the picture. You, in turn, will write a caption for your partner's drawing.*

Make sure each child has a partner. Explain to the children that they will have about 20 minutes to draw and another 20 minutes to write captions for each other's pictures.

As the children work: Ask them to leave about three inches at the bottom of their drawing for the caption. Encourage the children to make the pictures of themselves very large so that they fill up the paper. As they work, circulate and talk with the children about their drawings.

 (Continued Next Page)

Habits On Display ——————————————

When most of the children are ready to begin writing captions, list on the chalkboard words that they are likely to use, such as: *habit, behavior, adaptive, healthy, friendly,* etc. As they write, circulate and assist with spelling, syntax, and punctuation as necessary. Encourage the children to be creative.

Place and secure the finished art work on a wall or bulletin board, under the heading, "Habits On Display."

View the illustrations. As a group, give each artist credit for his or her work. Ask the writer to read his or her accompanying caption aloud, and give credit to the writer, too.

Conclude the activity. Thank the children for getting into the spirit of this activity with their drawings and captions.

A Letter to Me

A Writing Activity and Discussion

Relates to: Language Arts (oral language) and Drama, 4-6

Objectives:
The children will:
— identify personal behaviors required for success in school and family situations and habits and behaviors that hinder progress.
— demonstrate a positive attitude about self.

Note: This activity should follow the activity, "Habits On Display."

Time: approximately 30 minutes for writing and 10 minutes for sharing in dyads

Materials Needed: writing materials

Directions: **Introduce the activity.** Remind the children of previous activities having to do with habits. Point out that so far the activities have concentrated on examining their positive, helpful, *adaptive* habits. Gently suggest that they probably have some negative, unhelpful, *maladaptive* habits, too. Say: *Today we're going to talk to ourselves in writing about both kinds of habits. Write a letter to yourself. Do it as if you were someone else writing to you. First, tell yourself how good you feel about one or more of your good habits. Then, start a new paragraph and write to yourself about a habit you'd like to get rid of, or change. This is a chance to be very honest with yourself.*

When you finish your letter, find a partner and sit down together. Take turns reading your letters to each other. Your partner is the only person with whom you will be asked to share your letter.

Prior to the writing period: On the chalkboard, generate a list of words that the children are likely to use in their letters. This list of correctly spelled words might include *proud, habit, adaptive, maladaptive, eliminate, change*, etc.

 (Continued Next Page)

During the writing period: Circulate and assist the children with spelling, syntax, and punctuation, as needed.

Form dyads. When the children have completed their letters, have them form dyads and sit facing each other. (Be sure each child meets with a classmate who is a supportive friend.) Allow about five minutes for each partner to read his or her letter and discuss it with his or her partner.

Conclude the activity. Acknowledge the children for their self-honesty and thank them for their participation.

Habits Help or Hinder

Role Playing and Discussion

Relates to: **Drama and Language Arts (oral language) 4-6**

Objectives: The children will identify personal behaviors required for success in school and family situations, and habits and behaviors that hinder progress.

Time: approximately 40 minutes

Directions: **Introduce the activity.** In your own words suggest to the children: *Today we are going to dramatize some of the habits we've been talking about in previous activities—and maybe some we haven't mentioned yet.*

Let's make a list of the habits to be acted out. First, think of some positive, adaptive ones that help people in their lives. Then think of some negative, maladaptive ones that hinder people. As you call them out, I'll add them to the list.

On the chalkboard, write down at least three positive habits under the heading, "Adaptive Habits." Then do the same under the heading, "Maladaptive Habits."

Demonstrate. Ask the children which habit they would like to see dramatized. Offer to take the lead in the first dramatization, recruiting volunteers to assist you with supporting roles. Encourage the children to help you plan the dramatization. Then act it out. Afterward, ask the children:
— *What do you think of that habit?*
— *How does the habit affect the person who has it?*
— *How does the habit affect others?*

 (Continued Next Page)

Dramatize additional habits. Alternate between adaptive and maladaptive habits. Select an individual child to lead each dramatization. Help the leader plan the dramatization and play the role of the person with the habit. Allow the leader to recruit supporting actors from among the group. Enact the scene. (Expect hilarity when the maladaptive habits are dramatized.) After each dramatization, ask the children the same discussion questions you asked following your demonstration.

Lead a summary discussion. After all of the dramatizations have been completed and discussed, ask the children:
— *How can a person get rid of or change a maladaptive behavior?*

From the children's responses, try to generate a series of steps that a person might follow when trying to eliminate or change a maladaptive behavior. They might include:

1. Admit that you have the maladaptive habit.

2. Decide to replace it with a new, adaptive habit.

3. Really want to change.

4. Practice the new habit until the old one has been eliminated.

Conclude the activity. Thank the children for doing such a fine job of acting, thinking, speaking, and listening.

PROBLEM SOLVING AND DECISION MAKING

Making decisions and solving problems are things we all must do. Being able to make good decisions and to solve problems in ways that benefit ourselves and others are important skills that shape the quality of our lives now and in the future. This section contains activities that explore the ways we make decisions and solve problems and introduce processes for effectively doing both.

How Someone Else's Decision Affected Me ——— A Sharing Circle

Relates to: Language Arts (oral language) K-3

Objectives: The children will describe how decisions affect themselves and others.

Directions: **Review the sharing circle rules as necessary.**

State the topic. Say to the children: *We all make decisions every day. For instance, we decide what to wear and eat, how to act, what to do, and what to say. Many times, the decisions we make affect other people. At the same time, <u>other</u> people are making decisions too—and the decisions <u>they</u> make sometimes affect <u>us</u>. That is what we are going to talk about today. Our topic is, "How Someone Else's Decision Affected Me."*

Think of a decision that another person made that somehow affected you. Maybe someone in your family decided to bring ice cream home one night, and you were happy because you got to eat some of it. That decision had a good affect on you. On the other hand, maybe you have a friend whose family decided to move to another town and now you can't play with your friend anymore. That decision had a bad affect on you. Perhaps your older brother or sister decided to get a paper route, and now you spend a lot of time helping him or her fold papers. Or maybe your mother decided to work late at her office one evening, and you got very hungry waiting for her to come home and fix dinner. My decision to have a sharing circle today was just a little one, but it affected you because you are a member of the circle! When you tell us about the decision, be sure to describe how it affected you and how you felt about it. Think quietly for a moment or two, and raise your hand when you are ready. The topic is, "How Someone Else's Decision Affected Me."

(Continued Next Page)

How Someone Else's Decision Affected Me

Involve the children in sharing.

Conduct a summary. Ask these and other questions to generate a discussion:

— *What were some of the decisions that other people made that affected us?*

— *How did they affect us?*

— *Why do the decisions we make so often affect other people?*

— *Has anyone ever asked you to help make a decision because you would probably be affect by it? How did you feel about that?*

— *Would you like to help make decisions more often?*

— *How do you make decisions?*

Conclude the sharing circle.

Action Plan for Solving Problems

Experience Sheet and Discussion

Relates to: **Language Arts (listening, speaking, and writing) K-3**

Objectives: The children will identify simple strategies used in solving problems and making decisions.

Time: approximately 30 minutes for readiness, work time, and discussion

Materials Needed: a copy of the experience sheet, "Action Plan for Solving Problems," and a pencil for each child

Directions: **Introduce the activity.** Explain to the children that they can solve many problems by following a few easy steps. Describe a theoretical problem that *you* might have, such as: *Why are my houseplants turning yellow and dying?* Model the "Action Plan for Solving Problems" by following the steps in the template and writing them on the board.

1. Describe the problem in as much detail as possible. *The leaves on my houseplants started to turn yellow a month ago when we had such hot, dry weather. Even though I watered the plants everyday, the leaves got yellower until the plants began to die.*

2. List possible ways to solve the problem. *I could: 1) look in a book about plants to learn about plant care and diseases, 2) ask a friend for advice, 3) call a plant store or nursery and describe the problem, or 4) throw out the plants and start over.*

3. Choose the solution that seems best and try it out. If it works, terrific. If it doesn't, try another solution. *I asked a friend, and she said to give my plants more water. The plants died. I wonder if I gave the plants too much water? I think I'll look in a book on plant care.*

(Continued Next Page)

Action Plan for Solving Problems

Solve a second problem. After the children have helped you with your theoretical problem, ask them to think of a problem *they* might have. Follow the Action Plan once more, with their help. Again, record your actions on the board.

Ask the children to think of (and solve) the next problem with a partner. Distribute copies of the "Action Plan for Solving Problems," and ask the partners to fill out the steps. Walk around the room and offer assistance, as needed. Invite the children to share their completed Action Plans with the class.

Conclude the activity. Acknowledge the children for their problem-solving skills. Ask them:
— *Why is it important to know how to solve problems?*
— *How do you think this skill will help you in school? ...in a job when you are an adult?*

Action Plan For Solving Problems

Do you have a problem? Do you want to solve it? Follow these steps. See if you can come up with a good solution. Happy thinking!

<u>STEP 1.</u> Describe the problem. Who or what is part of the problem? What is or is not happening? How do you feel about the problem? List all the details of the problem.

<u>STEP 2:</u> List all of the possible ways to solve the problem—even if they seem silly. Remember, one of the solutions can be to "ask for help."

<u>STEP 3:</u> Choose the solution you think is best and try it out. If it works, congratulations! If it doesn't, try the next-best solution. Keep trying your solutions until you find one that works.

Decisions, Decisions, Decisions! ——

——— *Teacher Presentation and Discussion*

Relates to: Language Arts (listening and oral language) K-3

Objectives:	The children will: —identify alternatives in decision-making situations. —clarify personal beliefs and attitudes and how these affect decision-making.
Time:	approximately 30 minutes
Materials Needed:	chart paper and magic marker or chalkboard and chalk
Directions:	**Introduce the activity.** Say to the children: *We all make many decisions every day. Sometimes decisions are easy to make and sometimes they are hard. When they are hard, it helps to know some steps to take in making them. I'm going to read you a story about a girl who has a tough decision to make. Afterwards, let's see if we can figure out what she ought to do.* *Karen and Susan are friends. They sit next to each other at school. Karen is good at math. Susan doesn't like math, and has trouble with it. Tomorrow, their teacher is going to give the class a big math test. Susan comes up to Karen after school. She looks worried. She asks Karen if she can copy her answers on the test tomorrow. Karen doesn't say anything. But at home that night, she worries. She has to decide what to do.* **Give the children a few moments to think about the situation.** Then ask them: —*Why is Karen worried?* —*What decision does Karen have to make?* —*If Karen lets Susan copy her answers, what could happen?* —*If Karen says no, what could happen?* —*If Karen does nothing at all, what could happen?* —*If you were Karen, would you talk to someone before deciding? Who?* —*What decision do you think Karen should make?*

(Continued Next Page)

During the discussion, you and the children will no doubt name most of the steps in the decision-making process. As they are mentioned, write them on the chart paper.

1. **What is the decision about?** (definition)
2. **What are my choices?** (alternatives)
3. **What could happen if I make each choice?** (consequences)
4. **What is the best decision?**

Read through the steps with the children and discuss them. Then present additional decision-making situations. Ask the children to pretend that they are the person making the decision. Go through all of the steps together and then ask the children what decision they would make and why.

Sample Decision-Making Situations

Rick's uncle is visiting for the weekend. He wants to take Rick out exploring on a big boat. They will be gone all weekend. Rick would have to miss Little League practice. His team is getting ready for the play-offs. He has to make a decision.

Leah likes Carol better than any baby-sitter she's ever had. Carol plays games with Leah and her little brother. She reads to them, and is always nice. But last night, when Leah got up to go to the bathroom, she saw Carol pouring herself a glass of wine from the refrigerator. When Carol saw Leah watching, she seemed upset. She said, "Don't tell anyone, OK?"

Greg and Paul ask Ruben to ride his bike to the shopping mall with them. They offer to take him to a movie. Ruben really wants to go, but the brakes on his bike aren't working very well. He could probably make it, but he'd have to ride through heavy traffic. He has to decide what to do.

Conclude the activity. Thank the children for their participation and help with decision-making.

Thinking About Decisions

Experience Sheet and Discussion

Relates to: **Language Arts (reading, writing, and oral language) 4-6**

Objectives:
The children will:
— clarify personal beliefs and attitudes and how these affect decision-making.
— describe how decisions affect self and others.

Time: approximately 20 minutes

Materials Needed: a pencil and one copy of the experience sheet, "Thinking About Decisions," for each child

Directions: **Distribute the experience sheets.** Read the directions to the children while they read along silently. Talk about the different types of decisions and give an example of each.

Have the children complete the experience sheets.

Lead a discussion. Go over the list of decisions on the experience sheet and ask how many children placed each decision in each of the five categories. Discuss the reasons for their choices. Then ask volunteers to tell the group about some of their *own* decisions that they described at the bottom of the experience sheet. Ask these an other questions to facilitate further discussion:
— *Were most of your decisions automatic?*
— *Were many decisions out of your control?*
— *What kinds of decisions do you give a lot of thought?*
— *Which decisions were affected by your personal beliefs? Your attitudes?*
— *Which decisions were affected by your friends?*
— *Which decision were affected by your parents?*
— *Which decisions were affected by your interests?*

Conclude the activity. Thank the children for their contributions.

113

Thinking About Decisions

Everyone makes decisions daily. Some of the decisions are more important than others. Some are so important that they require lots of thought and study before a decision is made. Others are automatic. **Here are five categories for defining how decisions are made:**

0 = Not under my control   **3** = Think about it, but don't study it
1 = Automatic   **4** = Study it a little bit
2 = Sometimes think about it   **5** = Study it a lot

Below is a list of decisions. In front of each, put the number that stands for how *you* would make the decision:

_____To get up in the morning   _____What to eat and when
_____To tell the truth   _____To drink alcohol
_____What books to read   _____To study for a test
_____To say please and thank you   _____To use drugs
_____To stop at STOP signs   _____What career to have
_____To ride a bicycle   _____To go to school
_____Where to throw trash   _____What movie to see
_____To criticize a friend behind his or her back

Think back over the past week. On the lines below, describe some decisions you have made. Try to include one decision in each of these areas:
   • decisions about what to do   • health and safety decisions
   • decisions about school   • decisions about what is right and wrong
   • common, everyday decisions

_____

_____

_____

_____

_____

_____

_____

_____

Problem Solving With Literature

Relates to: Language Arts (listening and oral language) 4-6

Objectives: The children will identify problems and describe ways of dealing with them.

Note: This activity should precede the activity, "Creating T.V. Animations."

Time: as many 15- to 20-minute reading sessions as it takes to complete the book, plus one additional discussion period of approximately 20 minutes

Materials Needed: a copy of John Reynolds Gardiner's book, *Stone Fox*, illustrated by Maria Sewall (New York, Thomas Crowell, 1980).
Alternatives: *Where the Lilies Bloom* by Vera and Bill Cleaver (Philadelphia, Lippincott, 1969); *...and Now Miguel* by Joseph Krumgold (New York, Thomas Crowell, 1953)

Directions: **Introduce the activity.** Explain to the children that sometimes children have to work to help solve family financial problems. Ask them to think of a time when they or a young person whom they know had to help out by working. Tell them that you are going to read a book in which a ten-year-old boy does the job of an adult to help save his sick grandfather's farm. Ask them to listen to find out how he does it.

Read the book to the children. *Stone Fox* is the story of a young boy who lives with his grandfather. He tries to keep his grandfather's farm going by hitching his dog to a plow and havesting a crop of potatoes, only to learn that they owe ten years' back taxes. The boy enters a dogsled race and stakes everything on the hope that he will win against the best racers in the country, including the legendary Stone Fox. He nearly loses the race, but is saved by his most formidable opponent.

(Continued Next Page)

Problem Solving With Literature

Lead a discussion. After reading the book, ask these and other open-ended questions to help the children focus on what they learned from the story:

— *Why do you think grandfather became so ill?*

— *Why do you think little Willy took the responsibility of harvesting the potato crops with his dog, Searchlight?*

— *Why didn't little Willy accept the help of one of grandfather's friends in harvesting the crop?*

— *Why didn't little Willy want to go live with Doc Smith and let Mrs. Peacock take care of his grandfather?*

— *What would little Willy have done if he had not entered the dog sled race?*

— *Why did Stone Fox decide to help little Willy instead of winning the race and saving his own reputation?*

— *What would you have done if you were little Willy?*

— *What would you have done if you were Stone Fox?*

Conclude the activity. Thank the children for being such good listeners and thinkers.

Relates to: Language Arts and Art, 4-6

Objectives: The children will identify problems and describe ways of dealing with them.

Note: This activity should follow the activity, "Problem Solving With Literature."

Time: approximately 1 hour

Materials Needed: for each student: a 1-yard length of adding-machine tape and one piece of tagboard (cut about 6 inches long and 2 inches wider than the adding-machine tape), colored pencils or fine-tipped colored markers, and 2 pencils or small dowels

Directions: **Introduce the activity.** Explain to the children that they are going to make their own television animation versions of the *Stone Fox* story (or one of the alternate books from the previous activity).

Brainstorm the main events of the story. As the children name each event, write it on the chalkboard.

Sequence the events. Have each child select the eight to ten events that he or she considers the most important and put them in sequential order. Ask the children to share their lists with a partner to check for correctness. Lend the *Stone Fox* book to any children who do not sequence their chosen events in the correct order.

Create the T.V. animation versions of the story. Ask the children to develop their miniature television-cartoon shows by illustrating each of the main events in the story on adding machine tape. Distribute the materials and give the children the following instructions, demonstrating each step:

1. Draw a square television "screen" in the middle of the tagboard. Make its sides slightly smaller than the width of the adding-machine tape. (If you prefer, make a template of the square and distribute copies of the template for the children to trace.)

 (Continued Next Page)

2. Cut out the screen and draw the details of a television around the opening.

3. Draw a vertical line about 1-inch from each edge of the tagboard and slightly longer than the width of the tape. Cut along these lines to make slits through which to feed the tape into the back of the T.V. screen and out the other side.

4. Divide the tape into square frames the size of the screen. Leave a few inches of blank space at both ends of the tape.

5. Draw the events of the story in sequence on the frames.

6. Write a caption or use speech bubbles on each frame.

7. Thread the tape through the TV frame. Attach the pencils or dowels to the ends of the tape. Role and unroll the tape as the frames are pulled forward and rewound.

Give the children an opportunity to share their television shows with other students in the school. Invite another class into the room and pair each visitor with a student in your class so that the miniature T.V.s can be shared individually.

Lead a discussion. Ask the children a few speculative questions about how the story might continue:
— *What will little Willy do next to help his grandfather?*
— *What might his grandfather do next to help little Willy?*
— *What will happen to Stone Fox?*

Then ask a reflective questions or two, such as:
— *Do you think it is important for members of a family to help one another solve problems? Why?*

Conclude the activity. Thank the children for their excellent thinking and creative efforts.

How I Helped a Friend Solve a Problem — A Sharing Circle

Relates to: Language Arts (oral language) 4-6

Objectives:

The children will describe ways in which working together can overcome problems.

Directions:

Review the sharing circle rules as necessary.

State the topic. Say to the children: *When it comes to solving problems, sometimes two heads are better than one. We're going to talk about times like this in today's circle. The topic is, "How I Helped a Friend Solve a Problem."*

We all get into a jam from time to time and need the help of others. Think of a time when you helped a friend solve a problem that he or she couldn't solve alone. Perhaps your friend wanted to go on a bike ride with the scouts but didn't have a bike, so you lent him yours for the day. Maybe your class got a new student who didn't know anyone, so you were friendly to her and introduced her to others in the room. Have you ever had friends who were angry at each other and had a fight, and you helped them make up? What about a classmate who just couldn't remember the multiplication tables, so you worked with him after school with flashcards? Perhaps you helped a friend find her lost dog. Think of a time you helped a friend who was in a jam or had a problem. What kinds of feelings did you have in the situation? I'll give you a few minutes to reflect and come up with something to share. Look at me when you're ready. The topic is, "How I Helped a Friend Solve a Problem."

Involve the children in sharing.

Conduct a summary. Encourage the children to talk about what they learned in the circle. Ask these and other open-ended questions:
— *Why do we need to work together to solve problems?*
— *How do you feel when you have helped someone solve a problem?*
— *How can we avoid forcing our help on someone who doesn't want it?*

Conclude the sharing circle.

119

Steps for Solving a Problem

Experience Sheet and Discussion

Relates to: Language Arts (reading and oral language) 4-6

Objectives:

The children will:
—identify and assess problems that interfere with attaining one's goals.
—identify simple strategies used in solving problems.
—identify alternatives in decision-making situations.

Time:

approximately 40 to 45 minutes

Materials Needed:

a pencil and one copy of the experience sheet, "Steps for Solving a Problem" for each child

Directions:

Distribute the experience sheet to the children. Explain that you and the children are going to read and discuss the experience sheet together. Suggestions for how to present the concepts in the experience sheet follow:

Read "**Step One**" aloud to the children as they read along silently. Ask for general comments. Then, ask the children these questions to help facilitate a discussion:
—*Do you agree that people have to solve their own problems? What can happen if people try to solve other peoples' problems and ignore their own?*
—*Do you agree that it doesn't help to blame someone else for causing a problem that is yours? Have you ever had someone blame you for causing his or her problem? Did it help the person solve it?*

Ask two or three children to describe times when they were blamed for the problems of others—*without* identifying the parties involved.

Read "**Step Two**" with the children. Describe a problem of your own that you feel comfortable sharing with them. Then, with the assistance of the children, write a specific, clarifying statement of your problem on the chalkboard.

120   (Continued Next Page)

Read "**Step Three**" aloud to the children while they read along silently. Then discuss ways in which other people can be helpful in solving problems. Emphasize that the children can help the "helper" by asking him or her to (1) listen; (2) make suggestions; and (3) avoid criticism. Tell the children they were a big help to you when they listened to you describe your problem.

Next, read "**Step Four**." Describe to the children two or three possible solutions to your problem. Write these on the chalkboard. Then ask the children for their suggestions, writing them on the chalkboard as well.

Read "**Step Five**." Systematically discuss each alternative solution to your problem. Read each one and then ask aloud: *What will be the outcome for me and for the other people involved if I decide on this solution?*

Read "**Step Six**" aloud as the children read along silently. Tell them that the time has come to make a decision about how to solve your problem. State your decision. Describe any aspects of the decision that are uncomfortable, but stress that a decision has to be made and this seems like the best one to you right now.

Proceed to "**Step Seven**." Explain that you are determined to stick to your decision, however if after a certain period of time, your decision doesn't seem to be working, you are willing to go back to the beginning and start the process again.

Read the final statement on the experience sheet. Ask the children for their comments and reactions.

Conclude the activity: Thank the children for their attention and help during this activity.

Extension: Have the children go through the same process again, this time solving a problem of their own.

Steps for Solving a Problem

Here are seven steps for solving a problem. Use them the next time *you* have a problem:

- **Step One:** *Decide if it is really <u>your</u> problem.*

If the problem bothering you is really someone else's, let that person solve it. On the other hand, if it *is* your problem, don't blame someone else for causing it. That won't work either. Say to yourself: *This is my problem and I will do my best to solve it.*

- **Step Two:** *Name and describe the problem.*

It helps to know exactly what the problem is. Try not to be confused by it. Writing down a description of the problem can help you understand it.

- **Step Three:** *Decide whether or not to go to someone for help.*

People who care about you can be very helpful when you ask them for assistance. But don't try to get a helper to solve your problem for you. Ask the helper to listen and make suggestions.

- **Step Four:** *Think of as many ways to solve the problem as you can.*

Ask yourself: *What are some things I could do about this?* It's a good idea to write down the ideas you come up with. That way you won't forget any of them before you make up your mind.

- **Step Five:** *Carefully think over each idea you come up with.*

For each idea, ask yourself: *What will happen to me and the other people involved if I try this idea?*

- **Step Six:** *Decide what to do.*

If you have done all of the steps before this one, your decision will probably be a good one. It may not be *easy*, but it stands a good chance of working.

- **Step Seven:** *Stick to the decision.*

Once you decide, give your decision a chance. Go with it for awhile to see if it is really the best decision. If the decision doesn't work, start over again. If the decision causes more problems, solve those too.

These are steps for solving a problem that successful and happy people use. But remember: problems are part of life. There's nothing wrong with you if you have a problem. The important thing is to solve your problems as well as you can!

How My Decision Affected Someone Else ——————— A Sharing Circle

Relates to: Language Arts (oral language) 4-6

Objectives:

The children will describe how decisions affect self and others.

Directions:

Review the sharing circle rules as necessary.

Introduce the topic. Say to the children: *Our topic for today is, "How My Decision Affected Someone Else." Have you ever made a decision and been aware that someone else was either helped or hurt by it? Maybe you made a new friend and decided to play with him or her practically every chance you got. How did your decision affect your new friend? How did it affect your old friends? Maybe you decided to go camping instead of to soccer or little league practice. How did that decision affect the other members of the team? Or maybe you decided to practice especially hard for a music or dance recital, or a karate demonstration. How did that decision affect your teacher? ...your parents? Other people are affected by the things we do, and also by the things we say. So being polite and telling the truth affect others— and so do being impolite and telling lies. Think about it for a few moments. Tell us about a decision you made, but concentrate on describing the affect your decision had on others. When you are ready to share, raise your hand. The topic is, "How My Decision Affected Someone Else."*

Involve the children in sharing.

Conduct a summary. When the children are finished sharing, encourage them to talk about what they learned in the circle. Use these and other open-ended questions to spark a discussion:
— *Why is it that so many of our decisions affect others?*
— *Can you think of any types of decisions that don't affect others?*
— *When should you think about the affects of a decision—before you make it or after you make it?*

Conclude the sharing circle.

Making A Good Decision

Experience Sheet and Discussion

Relates to: **Language Arts (reading, writing, and oral language) 4-6**

Objectives: The children will use decision-making skills to set priorities, develop personal goals, and determine preferences.

Time: approximately 15 minutes to introduce the activity, 20 minutes to complete the experience sheet, and 10 minutes for a follow-up discussion

Materials Needed: a pencil and one copy of the experience sheet, "Decisions, Decisions!" for each child

Directions: **Distribute the experience sheets.** Read through the decision-making steps with the children, clarifying each one. Here are some ideas to discuss and questions to ask the children:

- Knowing what is important to you and what you want to accomplish involves such things as likes/dislikes, values, and interests. Most important, it involves having goals.

- You can get information by talking to people, visiting places, watching T.V., and reading. Once you have the information, you must be able to evaluate it. *If two people tell you to do opposite things, how are you going to know which is right? What if neither is right?*

- Look into the future. Ask yourself what would happen if you chose each of the alternatives available. For example, what would happen if:
  — *you did not go to college?*
  — *you never got married?*
  — *you ran away from home?*
  — *you dropped out of school?*
  — *you became a professional rock singer?*
  — *How did you make your predictions? What information did you use?*

124   (Continued Next Page)

Making A Good Decision

- When you reach the decision point, don't freeze up. If you've done a good job on the other steps, you can choose the best alternative with confidence. Remember, if you *don't* choose, someone else may choose for you.

- Not every decision requires an action plan, but the big ones usually do. The decision to visit your grandparents in another state next summer won't come true unless you make it. And that means *more* decisions. *Can you think what they are?*

Give the children time to complete the experience sheet. As they work, circulate and offer assistance. (To allow more time, let the children complete the experience sheet as homework.)

Have the children choose partners. Ask them to take turns sharing their decision and decision-making process.

Lead a discussion. Gather the children together and encourage them to talk about what they learned from the activity. Ask these and other questions:
— *What did you learn about decision-making from this activity?*
— *What can happen if you put off making a decision?*
— *Why is it important to know your interests and values when making decisions?*
— *How can having goals help you make decisions?*

Conclude the activity. Thank the children for their participation.

Decisions, Decisions!

The decision-making process involves <u>using what you know</u> (or can learn) <u>to get what you want</u>. Here are some steps to follow when you have a decision to make:

1. Define the decision to be made.
2. Know what is important to you and what you want to accomplish.
3. Study the information you already have. Get and study new information, too.
4. Look at each alternative and ask yourself what will happen to you and the other people involved if you choose it.
5. Make a decision.
6. Develop a plan for putting your decision into action.

What do you want?

Think of a decision that you need to make. Write a description of it here:

_____

_____

_____

Now follow steps **2** through **6**. Use these lines for your notes:

_____

_____

_____

_____

_____

_____

_____

DEVELOPING RESPECT FOR SELF AND OTHERS

The activities in this section help students to see that no two people are exactly alike. The point is gently made that, because each human being is unique, he or she is very special and has great value. Students are thus assisted to respect and value themselves and others as well.

Someone Liked What I Did ———

Relates to: Language Arts (oral language) K-3

Objective: The children will describe how a person's behavior influences the feelings and actions of others.

Directions: **Review the sharing circle rules as necessary.**

State the topic. In your own words, tell the children: *Today our topic is, "Someone Liked What I Did." Think about something you did that one or more people liked. It could have been here at school or it could have been somewhere else. Maybe you did something that made one of your parents feel proud of you. Or maybe you shared something with a friend in your neighborhood. Perhaps you were polite to someone at church, or somewhere else, and the person really liked it. Think about it and look up at me when you are ready to speak and listen. Our topic is, "Someone Liked What I Did."*

Involve the children in sharing.

Conduct a summary. Here are four questions to ask the children. Allow them to answer in a free-flowing discussion:
—*We did things people liked. How could we tell they liked the things we did?*
—*Does it do us any good to do things other people like?*
—*How can you show a person that you like what he or she does?*
—*How can you tell if you do something someone doesn't like?*

Conclude the sharing circle

How Terry Trout Learned to Like Himself

A Big Classroom Book

Relates to: Language Arts (reading and oral language) K-3

Objectives: The children will demonstrate positive attitudes about themselves.

Note: This is the first of two sequential activities designed to help the children understand that it is okay for them to have a positive attitude about themselves.

Time: approximately 20 to 30 minutes

Materials Needed: for making a classroom book: large sheets of sturdy paper (18 inches by 14 inches or larger) and a black magic marker for use in lettering the cover, title page 3, and text of the story; a hand mirror at least in 5 inches in diameter

Directions: **Preparations:** Prepare a classroom book with no illustrations. (These will be produced by the children in the next activity.)

In a large manuscript style, print the following lines (or your own creative variation) on each page:

Cover: How Terry Trout Learned to Like Himself
Inside cover: By (The Children of Room 8) and (Your Name); place; and date.
Page 1: Terry Trout is a fish.
Page 2: He is a fine fish.
Page 3: He can eat worms.
Page 4: He can swim fast.
Page 5: He can play "school" with the other fish.
Page 6: But Terry doesn't know that he is a fine fish.
Page 7: One day he sees Sally Salmon. He says, "I wish I were a fine fish like you."
Page 8: Sally Salmon laughs. She says, "You <u>are</u> a fine fish."
Page 9: But fish don't have mirrors. Terry can't see himself. He doesn't believe Sally Salmon.
Page 10: One day Terry sees a fly on top of the water. It looks so good!
Page 11: He jumps to catch it.
Page 12: Up, up, up he goes!

(Continued Next Page)

Page 13: Terry jumps so high, he pops out of the water! What do you think he sees?

Page 14: Terry sees his reflection. He sees himself.

Page 15: Terry says, "Sally Salmon was right!"

Page 16: "I am a fine fish!"

Gather the children together. In your own words, tell them: *I know a very good story about a little fish and I'd like to tell it to you. Would you like to hear the story?* (The children respond.) *OK. The name of this story is "How Terry Trout Learned to Like Himself."*

Briefly tell the children the first part of the story in your own words to supply them with an introduction. Then announce: *I wrote the story in a big classroom book, but there is something the classroom book doesn't have. It needs illustrations, so later on today (or tomorrow) we will make some pictures for it. But, for now, let's look at the classroom book and read the story together.*

Beginning with the cover, read the story. Ask the children to listen and read along silently as you display the classroom book and read the story to them. With a sweeping movement of your free hand, indicate which words you are reading.

See if the children can guess the ending. At the end of page 13, ask the children: *How do you think this story is going to end?* Listen to their ideas and then read the ending. Discuss how Terry Trout sees himself in the surface of the pond when he is out of the water and how he comes to realize that he *is* a fine fish. This causes him to like himself.

Bring out a mirror. Tell the children that people can see themselves in mirrors and realize what fine people they are. People can like themselves, too! Allow the children to view their reflections. Tell each one: *See what a fine girl (or boy) you are!* Seek agreement from the child either through words, or facial expressions. Expect laughter, but do not allow derisive laughter.

Conclusion: Ask the children to read the story with you in unison once or twice. Thank them for being such good readers, speakers, and listeners. Tell the children that you are looking forward to helping them make illustrations for the story later on.

In the next activity, the children create illustrations for this classroom book.

Illustrating the "Terry Trout" Story —

Art, Reading, & Discussion

Relates to: Art and Language Arts (reading and oral language) K-3

Objective: The children will demonstrate positive attitudes about themselves.

Note: This activity is the second of two sequential activities designed to help the children realize that it is okay to like themselves.

Time: approximately 30 minutes for assigning and making illustrations, and 15 to 20 minutes for viewing and reading the completed Big Book

Materials Needed: The classroom book, *How Terry Trout Learned to Like Himself*, sturdy art paper in pastel colors (11 inches by 24 inches or larger), crayons, and glue

Directions: **Introduce and organize the activity.** Remind the children of the group's agreement to illustrate the classroom book. Explain: *We have many different pages to illustrate. Each page shows a different scene in the story, and each page needs a picture. Let's decide who will make each picture.*

Open the classroom book. Turn to page 1 and read it to the children. Next, have the children read it with you in unison. Then ask, *What should the picture for this page look like?* Listen and validate any suggestions that the children make. Finally, ask for a volunteer to make the illustration for that page. Continue in this manner until each page has been read, ideas for a picture have been discussed, and an illustrator has been assigned. (As assignments are made, jot down who is illustrating each page so that you can make reminders and avoid mix-ups later.)

If some children are left without an assignment, have them create pictures for the cover, title page, "The end" page, inside of the back cover, and back cover. Additional illustrations can be made into posters "advertising" the story.

By this time the children will probably be eager to start.

 (Continued Next Page)

As the children work: Assist them with their illustrations only as absolutely necessary. Encourage them to make the fish, worms, flies, and other items in their pictures very big, so that they fill up the whole paper and can be seen when the classroom book is read by the group.

Circulate and talk with the children about their drawings. Make positive comments: *Look at the big eyes Bobby drew on his picture of Terry. And who is this, Sally Salmon?*

When the children finish their illustrations, help each child place and secure his or her picture to the correct page in the classroom book.

View the illustrations in the classroom book. After the illustrations have been added to the classroom book, look at and enjoy them with the children, one at a time. Without reading the story, focus on each illustration and admire it together. Give each illustrator credit for his or her fine art work. Then read the classroom book to the children as they read along silently. Finally, ask them to read it with you in unison.

Conclusion. Thank the children for drawing such fine illustrations for the classroom book.

A Day With Hector Penguin

Reading, Discussion, and Art

Relates to: Art and Language Arts (literature and oral language) K-3

Objectives: The children will describe how all persons need to belong and be accepted and respected by others.

Time: approximately 15 to 20 minutes

Materials Needed: a copy of the book *Hector Penguin*, by Louise Fatio, illustrated by Roger Duvolsin (New York, McGraw-Hill, 1973); sheets of construction paper (two per child); tongue depressors; scissors; and glue

Directions: **Preparation.** Draw two 3-inch circles on each sheet of construction paper.

Read *Hector Penguin* to the children. The story tells of a penguin who finds himself in a forest full of animals who have never seen a penguin before. The animals tease and scold him because he is different. A worldly-wise crow eventually educates the other animals regarding the wonderful capabilities of penguins. Hector's self-esteem is restored and he is accepted into the group.

Discuss the story. Ask these and other questions to help stimulate a discussion of the story:

— *How did Hector feel when each of the animals in the forest refused to include him as one of its kind?*
— *How did he feel when the crow informed the other animals about a penguin's capabilities?*
— *How did Hector feel when he was finally accepted by the group?*

(Continued Next Page)

A Day With Hector Penguin — (Continued)

Art project. Have the children go to their tables and cut out the two 3-inch circles that you have drawn on their construction paper. Tell them to draw a happy face on one of their circles, and a sad face on the other. Then have the children glue their circles to the end of a tongue depressor, so that the happy face shows on one side and the sad face shows on the other. Explain that you are going to read the book again, and that the children are going to use the faces to show how Hector Penguin feels in various parts of the story.

After clean-up, gather the children around for a re-reading of *Hector Penguin*. Make sure that the children are holding their happy/sad-face puppets. Ask them to hold up the sad-face side when they think Hector feels sad in the story, and the happy-face side when they think Hector feels happy. While reading, pause at appropriate times to cue the children to hold up their puppets. Thank the children for helping you read the story again.

Extension: For additional read-alouds, the following books relate to the theme of belonging and acceptance in a school setting: *Will I Have a Friend?*, written by Miriam Cohen and illustrated by Lillian Hoban (New York, MacMillan, 1967) is about a kindergarten boy who goes to school for the first time and worries that he won't have a friend, but finds one before the end of the school day. *Starring First Grade* by the same author-illustrator team (New York, Greenwillow, 1985) is about a first grader who is unhappy about the part he is assigned in the class play until he helps a classmate during a moment of stage fright and saves the performance.

"You Look Ridiculous" — Art and Drama

Relates to: Language Arts (literature and oral language), Science, and Art, K-3

Objectives: The children will:
—describe how all persons need to belong and to be accepted by others.
—identify how people are unique individuals.

Time: two sessions—approximately 1 hour the first day and 30 minutes the following day

Materials Needed: a copy of the book *You Look Ridiculous (Said the Rhinoceros to the Hippopotamus)*, written and illustrated by Bernard Waber (Boston, Houghton Mifflin, 1966); pictures of jungle animals mentioned in the book (lion, monkey, rhinoceros, elephant, and turtle); heavy butcher paper; crayons or marking pens; and scissors

Directions: **Read Bernard Waber's *You Look Ridiculous* to the children.** It tells of a hippopotamus who is informed by a rhinoceros that she looks ridiculous without a horn on the end of her nose. So she goes around asking all the other animals if they think she looks ridiculous. They all agree that she does, but for different reasons. The hippo then dreams of having the rhino's horn, the lion's mane, spots like the leopard's, the giraffe's neck, the turtle's shell, and a voice like the nightingale's. She soon realizes that she really *does* look ridiculous with all these characteristics and decides to accept herself just as she is.

As the various animals are introduced into the story, ask the children to predict what each one will say is needed by the hippo. When you have finished reading, talk about the need of the children and other people to be accepted just as *they* are, not as others think they should be.

Hold up the pictures of the animals and ask the children to point out the characteristics of each animal that make it unique. Have the children suggest other animals and name their obvious physical traits too.

Let the children each choose one of the animals and draw a picture of it on butcher paper, using crayons or marking pens. Allow the animal paintings to dry overnight. The next day, have the children cut out their animals. Reread Waber's book. Finally, have groups of children hold up and speak the part of their animal as you informally read or tell the story a third and final time.

Display the animal drawings on the bulletin board.

135

Mirror Motions —————— *A Movement Activity*

Relates to: Physical Education and Social Studies, K-3

Objectives: | The children will demonstrate desirable skills for interacting with and relating to others.

Time: | approximately 30 minutes

Materials Needed: | full-length mirror, and one colored scarf per student (optional)

Directions: | **Introduce the activity.** Place the full-length mirror so that it is facing the children. Ask a volunteer to stand in front of the mirror and demonstrate several slow movements. Tell the other children to notice how the "person" in the mirror does exactly what the person in front of the mirror is doing. Explain that each child will face a partner and do a similar activity called "The Mirror Game."

Divide the children into pairs. Tell them that in this activity one child will be the leader and the other will be the mirror. Just like the reflection in the mirror, the person playing the "mirror" must do exactly what the person outside the mirror is doing. Emphasize that the partners must always face each other and the leader needs to move very slowly so that the partner can follow him/her just like a reflection in a mirror. Have the children begin with hand movements only. Then add head, shoulders, leg, and body movements. After a few minutes, announce that the partners must change places so that the "mirror" becomes the person and the person is the "mirror."

Next, have the children sit on the floor, forming circles of five to six children each. Ask one child to be the leader. Instruct the leader to do slow movements with his/her head, shoulders, hands, arms, and legs, while maintaining contact with the floor. Once again, the other children will mirror the leader's movements. Let each child be the leader for about 1 to 2 minutes.

136

(Continued Next Page)

Mirror Motions ——————————— *(Continued)*

Play a similar mirroring game outdoors or in an auditorium, using scarves (optional). Bring all of the children together as a single group and give each child a scarf. Let one child at a time be the leader in front of the whole group, while everyone else plays the part of a mirror. Make sure that there is plenty of space between the children so that they can swing the scarves with large, sweeping movements.

Conclusion. Ask the children the following questions to generate a discussion of the activity:

— *Did you have fun doing the activity?*
— *Which did you enjoy most, being the mirror or the leader?*
— *How did you feel when the mirror followed your movements?*
— *How did you feel when the mirror did not follow your movements?*
— *How does cooperating and taking turns show respect for others?. . . for yourself?*

My Dad Was the New Kid

A Big Classroom Book

Relates to: **Language Arts (reading and oral language) K-3**

Objectives:

The children will:
—explain the importance of showing respect for others.
—describe how all persons need to belong and be accepted by others.

Note: This is the first of three sequential activities designed to help the children develop empathy and respect for others. Specifically, the children become more aware of how they can affect the feelings of others by accepting and including them.

Time:

approximately 20 to 30 minutes

Materials Needed:

for making a big classroom book: large sheets of sturdy paper (at least 18 inches by 24 inches) and a black magic marker for lettering the cover, title page, and text of the story

Directions:

Preparation: Prepare a big classroom book with no illustrations. (These will be produced by the children in the next activity.)

In manuscript printing, write the following on each page:

Cover: My Dad Was the New Kid
Inside cover: By (The Children of Room 14) and (Your Name), place, and date
Page 1: When Tommy came to school today he got a surprise. There was a new kid in his class.
Page 2: The teacher gave the new kid a desk right next to Tommy's desk.
Page 3: "Hello," said the new kid. "My name is David. What's yours?"
Page 4: "Tommy," came the answer. Tommy said nothing more. After that he did not look at David.

     (Continued Next Page)

Page 5: That night Tommy told his family about the new kid. "He bothers me," said Tommy.

Page 6: "I was the new kid so many times," said Tommy's Dad. "My family moved again and again. Every time we moved I had to make new friends or have no friends at all."

Page 7: "No kidding, Dad?" said Tommy. "I didn't know that!"

Page 8: "No kidding," said Tommy's Dad. "It was hard on me. Sometimes the kids in the new school weren't friendly. Other times I got lucky and a boy or girl would talk to me, or invite me to join a game."

Page 9: "Why didn't you just talk to them?" asked Billy.

Page 10: "Well son, I did," answered Tommy's Dad. " But it felt so much better when they talked to me. I needed to know they liked me. I was the new kid."

Page 11: "I'll never forget how good I felt when a boy or girl was friendly," Tommy's Dad said. "It meant so much to me. Were you friendly to the new kid in your class, Tommy?"

Page 12: "No," said Tommy. "He bothered me. But maybe the reason was because he was new."

Page 13: "That's probably right," said Tommy's Dad. "What are you going to do tomorrow?"

Page 14: "When I see him tomorrow I'll say, 'Hi David,'" answered Tommy. "Then I will talk to him. I'll even invite him to play with me and my friends at recess."

Page 15: "Good for you, son," said Tommy's Dad. "I'm proud of you."

Page 16: Tommy smiled at his Dad and said, "I'm glad you told me you were the new kid, Dad. Now I know how he feels."

Gather the children together. In your own words, show them the classroom book and tell them: *I have a story I'd like to read to you. It's about a boy named Tommy who feels bothered when a new kid shows up in his class. The new kid wants to be accepted and included, but Tommy doesn't feel like being friendly. As I read the story, you will notice the pages have no pictures. Later,*

(Continued Next Page)

My Dad Was the New Kid —— (Continued)

we can illustrate them. Soon we will have a sharing circle and talk about how each of us, at one time or another, has accepted and included another person.

Beginning with the cover, read the story. Ask the children to listen and read along silently as you display the classroom book and read the story to them.

Discuss the turning points in the story with the children. At the end of page 5, ask the children: *What do you think Tommy's Dad is going to say to Tommy?* And at the end of page 13, ask them: *What do you think Tommy is going to say?* Listen to their ideas and then read the ending.

Discuss the natural feelings people have when they meet others for the first time. It's normal to feel uneasy, like Tommy did, around someone new. It's also normal for the new person to want to be accepted and included. When Tommy's Dad tells him how he remembers feeling like the "new kid," Tommy begins to care about David's feelings because he cares for his Dad. His Dad's story helps him realize how important it is for him to be friendly to David the next day.

Ask the children to read the story with you in unison once or twice.

Conclude the activity. Thank the children for being such good readers, speakers, listeners, and thinkers. Tell them you are looking forward to seeing the illustrations they make for the story.

Illustrating the "New Kid" Story

Art, Reading, and Discussion

Relates to: Art and Language Arts (reading and oral language) K-3

Objectives:

The children will describe how all persons need to belong and be accepted by others.

Note: This is the second of three activities designed to help the children develop empathy and respect. Specifically, the children become more aware of how they can affect the feelings of others by accepting and including them.

Time:

approximately 30 minutes for assigning and making illustrations, and 15 to 20 minutes for viewing and reading the completed classroom book

Materials Needed:

the classroom book prepared in the previous activity, sturdy art paper in pastel colors (at least 11 inches by 24 inches in size), and crayons

Directions:

Introduce and organize the activity. Remind the children of the group's agreement to illustrate the classroom book, "My Dad Was the New Kid." Explain: *We have lots of different pages to illustrate. Each one will show a different scene in the story. Let's think of some creative ideas and decide who will make each picture.*

Open the classroom book. Turn to page 1, read it to the children, and have them to read it with you in unison. Ask, *What should the picture for this page look like?* Listen and validate the children's suggestions. Then ask for a volunteer to make the illustration. Continue in this manner until each page has been read, ideas for an illustration have been discussed, and an illustrator has been assigned. (Jot down who is illustrating each page, in order to make reminders and avoid mix-ups later.)

If some children are left without an assignment, explain that their pictures will be used for the cover, title page, "The end" page, inside of the back cover, and back cover. Posters "advertising" the story can be made with any additional illustrations.

     (Continued Next Page)

Illustrating the "New Kid" Story

Have the children complete their illustrations. Assist them only as absolutely necessary. Encourage them to make the people in their pictures large enough to fill up the entire sheet of paper.

Make positive comments as you circulate among the children. *See how Sharon drew Tommy's eyes to show he isn't even looking at David. ...That's very creative, Sean. You're showing Tommy and his Dad talking as they take a walk together.* Encourage children who can write to make cartoon bubbles containing the words the characters are speaking.

When the children finish their illustrations, place and secure them on the appropriate pages of the classroom book.

View the illustrations in the classroom book. After the illustrations have been added to all parts of the classroom book, look at them with the children Without reading the story, focus on each illustration and admire it together. Give the illustrator credit for his or her fine art work. Then read the classroom book to the children while they read along silently. Finally, ask them to read it with you in unison.

Conclude the activity. Thank the children for drawing such fine illustrations for the classroom book.

A Time I Accepted and Included Someone ——

Someone —————— A Sharing Circle

Relates to: Language Arts (oral language) K-3

Objectives: The children will describe how all persons need to belong and be accepted by others.

Note: This is the third of three activities designed to help the children develop empathy and respect for others. In the environment of the sharing circle, the children relate instances in which they demonstrated accepting and inclusive behavior toward others.

Directions: **Review the sharing circle rules as necessary.**

State the topic. In your own words, tell the children: *We've been talking about how much people want to be treated in friendly ways by others. Everyone needs to feel liked, and most everyone wants to be invited to play or participate with others. Yet sometimes it's hard for us to accept a new person. So today, let's talk about times we were friendly to someone who needed our friendship—even if it felt uncomfortable. Our topic is, "A Time I Accepted and Included Someone."*

Can you remember a time like that? It could have been anywhere— here at school, in your neighborhood, or at church. Perhaps someone new came along and you were nice to that person because you knew how he or she felt. Maybe you were the new person yourself once, and you remembered how much you wanted to be accepted and included at that time. Or maybe the person you accepted and included was someone you'd had a disagreement with, and he or she needed to know you still liked him or her.

If you decide to share, tell us how you let the person know that you accepted and wanted to include him or her. Think about it for a few moments. When you are ready, look up at me and we'll start the session. The topic is, "A Time I Accepted and Included Someone."

Involve the children in sharing.

Conduct a summary. Here are three questions to ask the children. Use them to generate a free-flowing discussion:
—*Does it mean a lot to people when we accept and include them?*
—*Why is it hard sometimes to show someone acceptance and to include him or her?*
—*Did anyone get any ideas for ways to treat someone when you want to accept and include him or her?*

Conclude the sharing circle.

143

Ways to Make and Keep Friends ─────

───────────── ***Role Playing and Discussion***

Relates to: Drama and Language Arts (oral language) K-3

Objectives: | The children will:
—describe how all persons need to belong and be accepted by others.
—demonstrate desirable skills for interacting with and relating to others.
—demonstrate respect for others.

Time: | approximately 30 minutes

Directions: | **Introduce the activity.** In your own words say to the children: *We all need to be treated in friendly ways. And one of the best ways to be treated well <u>ourselves</u> is to be a good friend to <u>others</u> and to treat <u>them</u> well. So let's talk about friendship today. Let's act out, and show one another, how friendship really works. To get started, let's make a list of some ways to make a friend—ways that work well. Then we'll make a list of ways to keep a friend.*

Under the heading, "Making Friends," list at least three strategies that the children describe. Do the same under the heading, "Keeping Friends." As each strategy is mentioned, discuss how ineffective it would be to do the opposite. For example, if a child says that to make a friend you need to introduce yourself and ask what the person's name is, you might say: *Right. Who would want to be friends with someone who calls you, "What's-your-name?"*

Demonstrate. Suggest to the children: *I've got some ideas for situations we can act out using the strategies on our lists. When I describe a situation, if you have an idea which strategy will work, raise your hand. If I call on you, come up in front of the group and act it out. If you want some other actors to help, you may call on them. Let me go first to show you what I mean. The first situation is: <u>You are at a friend's birthday party. One of your friend's cousins, who is your age, is there too—but you've never seen him before. How do you make friends with the cousin?</u>*

(Continued Next Page)

Ways to Make and Keep Friends ———

Ask volunteers to play the friend who is having the birthday, two or three children at the party (who are having a good time), and your friend's cousin. Tell the volunteers what you would like them to say and do. Then, dramatize the scene, introducing yourself to the cousin and demonstrating friendly behavior toward him or her. For example, you might offer to share the last piece of pizza with him, or pour her some punch when you refill your own glass. Afterward, ask the children: *What do you think of what I did to make friends with this person? How did he or she seem to like what I did?*

Choose volunteers to dramatize several additional scenarios. Help each one select a strategy and choose the appropriate number of actors. Assist with planning, as necessary. At the end of each dramatization hold a brief discussion with the entire group.

<u>**Possible scenarios for the "Making Friends" dramatizations:**</u>
1. You are playing a game with some of your friends in your front yard. A new girl in the neighborhood walks up and stands nearby watching.

2. The teacher asks you and a boy in your class whom you don't know very well to take a box of books to the library. You believe this boy is much smarter than you are.

3. A family of a different race moves into a house on your street. They have two children about your age. One day the children come out of the house just as you walk by on your way to school.

<u>**Possible scenarios for the "Keeping Friends" dramatizations:**</u>
1. Your friend telephones you, but you just sat down to dinner with your family and it isn't a good time to talk.

2. Your friend had a fight with her big sister and is feeling terrible.

3. You are at the movies with a friend. Just before the movie starts, another friend comes over and sits beside you and says, "Hi." These two friends of yours don't know each other.

A Time I Felt Left Out

A Sharing Circle

Relates to: Language Arts (oral language) 4-6

Objectives: The children will describe how all persons need to belong and to be accepted by others.

Note: This sharing circle should be conducted either before or soon after the movement activity, "Group Break In!"

Directions: **Review the sharing circle rules as necessary.**

State the topic. Say to the children: *The topic for this session isn't a happy one. It's, "A Time I Felt Left Out." At one time or another, all of us have been left out of something that we wanted to be included in. Maybe it was a game our friends were playing, or a job the family was doing at home, but felt you were too young to participate in. Possibly you weren't feeling well and couldn't go to school on a day everyone else was going on a field trip. Or maybe your friends were invited to a birthday party and you weren't. Whatever it was, you felt left out of what others were doing. Think about it for a few moments and, when you are ready, raise your hand. The topic is, "A Time I Felt Left Out."*

Involve the children in sharing.

Conduct a summary. Use these and other questions to stimulate a discussion of what was learned in the circle:
— *How did most of us feel about being left out?*
— *Why is it so important to us to feel included?*
— *What could you have done to be included?*
— *What can you do if you see that someone is being left out?*

Conclude the sharing circle.

Group Break In!

A Movement Activity

Relates to: Physical Education and Language Arts (oral language) 4-6

Objectives:

The children will:
—describe the importance of cooperation to accomplishing a task.
—describe what it is like to be excluded from a group.
—identify and describe ways of being included in a group.

Time:

approximately 30 to 40 minutes

Directions:

Preparation: Locate a large, open space where the children can move about freely and make noise.

Introduce the activity. Number the children off randomly to form groups of seven or eight. Say to them: *I am going to give you a task to perform as a group. One person will stand outside each group and try to break in, while the other children form a tight circle with their arms locked together to keep that person out. The person outside the circle must try his or her best to get inside the circle and the group must try equally hard to keep that person out. Don't make it easier for friends, and don't get lazy. Each of you will have a turn to be on the outside. When you are, you will have 2 minutes to talk or climb your way into the circle. When you succeed in breaking in, or when your time is up, you will become part of the circle and another person will take a turn on the outside.*

Start the activity. Expect lots of laughter and shouting. Be prepared for frustration on the part of the person trying to break in. Continue the game until all of the children have had an opportunity to be on the outside.

(Continued Next Page)

Group Break In! ———————— *(Continued)*

Lead a discussion. Gather the groups together and ask them to talk about the experience. Use these and other questions:

— *What did it feel like to be outside the group?*

— *What did it feel like to be part of the group?*

— *Did your group cooperate? What was your common purpose?*

— *As a group member, was it more difficult to keep a friend out than someone you didn't know quite so well?*

— *How did it feel to succeed at getting in? ...to fail?*

— *What were some of the ways you used to keep others out of the circle?*

— *What do we do to keep others out of our activities in real life?*

— *How has this experience changed your feelings about being included and excluded?*

Conclude the activity. Thank the children for their enthusiasm, determination, and cooperation.

Letters to David

Relates to: **Language Arts (writing and oral language) 4-6**

Objectives:

The children will:
— describe how all persons need to belong and to be accepted by others.
— demonstrate respect and understanding of differences among people's cultures, life styles, attitudes, and abilities.

Note: This is the first in a series of three activities having to do with making and keeping friends.

Time: approximately 45 minutes

Materials Needed: the "Letter from David;" writing materials for all of the children.

Directions: **Introduce the activity.** Tell the children that you would like to read them a letter written by a fifth grader who lives in another city.

Read the "Letter from David." When you have finished, ask the children what they think of the letter. Encourage them to discuss their reactions to David's experience. Then suggest: *Let's write letters to David and give him some advice. We can't mail the letters, because we don't know David's last name or address. But maybe by writing the letters, we can learn how to help other children in this situation whom we <u>do</u> know. What could we say to David that might help?*

 (Continued Next Page)

Letters to David

Jot down any suggestions on the chalkboard, including your own. For example:

- Start your letter by empathizing with David's feelings, maybe even telling him about a time when you were new and had similar feelings.
- Urge him to be patient. Sometimes other children aren't friendly because they need time to become acquainted with a new person.
- Suggest that David approach some of the other students and be friendly to them.
- Suggest that as soon as he does make a friend, he invite the friend to his house.
- Urge him to be friendly and patient and not to let the situation get him down.

Prior to the writing period: Generate a list of words that the children are likely to use in their letters. Write them on the chalkboard so that the children can check their spelling against the list.

During the writing period: Circulate and assist the children, as necessary.

After the writing period: Have the children form triads. Explain that each person will have three minutes to read his or her letter and discuss it with the other members of the triad. Begin the sharing period. At the end of three minutes, signal the children to move on to the second letter.

Conclude the activity: Collect the letters and display them around the room, along with the "Letter from David." Thank the children for their suggestions and participation.

Letter from David

Dear Tommy,

I'm a boy in the fifth grade. I'm also Puerto Rican.

My family moved and I just went to my new school for the first time today. There are hardly any Puerto Ricans in this new school.

I hated it. Everybody stared at me like I was from another planet. It seemed like they wished I hadn't joined their class and I felt the same way. I miss my friends at my old school so bad.

One student said Hi, but mostly people stayed away. I feel very lonely and sad. What would you do if you were me?

Sincerely,

David

Something I Never Do When I Want to Keep a Friend —————— A Sharing Circle

Relates to: Language Arts (oral language) 4-6

Objectives:

The children will:
— describe how all persons need to belong and to be accepted by others.
— demonstrate desirable skills for interacting with and relating to others.
— demonstrate tolerance and flexibility in group situations.
— demonstrate respect and understanding of differences among people's cultures, life styles, attitudes, and abilities.

Note: This is the second in a series of three activities having to do with making and keeping friends.

Directions:

Review the sharing circle rules as necessary.

State the topic. In your own words, say to the children: *Today we are going to talk about friendship. In the letters we wrote to David (previous activity), we suggested some things he could do to make friends with his new classmates. Now let's focus on how to <u>keep</u> our friends. Our topic is, "Something I Never Do When I Want to Keep a Friend."*

No one is a perfect friend. But we can certainly avoid doing things that might cause us to lose our friends. Has anyone ever treated you in a way that made you decide you didn't want to be friends with him or her anymore? If so, you know better than to treat your own friends that way. Maybe someone broke a promise that he or she made to you. Or maybe you told a secret to someone and then found out that he or she repeated your secret to several other people. Perhaps you had a friend who never asked you over, or didn't invite you to her birthday party. Or maybe you lent a video to someone and he never returned it. It's good to know what actions to avoid if you want to keep a friend. Think of an example and tell us about it, but don't mention any names. Take a few moments to think about it. When you are ready, raise your hand. The topic is, "Something I Never Do When I Want to Keep a Friend."

Involve the children in sharing.

Conduct a summary. Use these and other questions to generate a discussion of what was learned in the circle:
— *How would our friends feel if we treated them badly?*
— *Does a real friend care how you feel?*
— *How do you let your friends know that <u>you</u> care how <u>they</u> feel?*

Conclude the sharing circle.

A Real Friend Is . . .

Role Playing and Discussion

Relates to: Drama and Language Arts (oral language) 4-6

Objectives:

The children will:
— describe how all persons need to belong and to be accepted by others.
— demonstrate desirable skills for interacting with and relating to others.
— demonstrate tolerance and flexibility in group situations.
— demonstrate respect and understanding of differences among people's cultures, life styles, attitudes, and abilities.

Note: This is the third in a series of three activities having to do with making and keeping friends.

Time: approximately 40 minutes

Materials Needed: chalkboard and chalk or chart paper and magic markers

Directions:

Introduce the activity. In your own words suggest to the children: *We've been focusing our attention on how to make and keep friends. We've also discussed things we <u>don't</u> do when we want someone to stay friends with us. Today, let's act out some of the actions we've talked about and maybe some new ones we haven't thought of yet.*

Write the headings, "Friendly Actions" and "Unfriendly Actions" on the chalkboard or chart paper. Ask the children to help you list things that people do when they want to make friends with someone or keep a friendship going. Then ask them to help you list things that ruin friendships. Try to list at least three actions under each heading.

(Continued Next Page)

A Real Friend Is . . . ─────── *(Continued)*

Demonstrate. Select one of the behaviors from the "Friendly Actions" list. Ask volunteers to assist you with your dramatization. For example, if you are demonstrating the effects of being a good listener, you will need to have one of the children talk to you while you listen. Let the children help you plan the scene. Then act it out. Afterward, ask the children:
— *How did you feel as I listened to (Marlene)?*
— *How did my listening seem to affect her (or him)?*
— *How did (Marlene) seem to feel about me?*

Ask for volunteers to role play other items from the two lists. Help them plan their dramatizations. Allow a few minutes for rehearsals. Then have the children enact their scenes, one at a time. Expect strong reactions, especially amusement, when both friendly and unfriendly actions are dramatized. After each dramatization, ask the children the same discussion questions you asked after your demonstration.

Lead a summary discussion. After all of the dramatizations have been completed and discussed, write the following phrase on the chalkboard or chart paper:

A real friend is someone who...

Ask the children to finish the sentence. Record their sentence endings. Then write this next phrase on the chalkboard or chart paper and have the children complete it, too:

A real friend is someone who doesn't...

Conclude the activity. Thank the children for their fine acting, thinking, speaking, and listening.

APPRECIATING DIFFERENCES

Developing an understanding of the ways we are different from one another is the beginning of being able to appreciate these differences. Appreciating differences comes from seeing ways in which being different helps us make greater contributions and from learning that the ways we are different are often the ways that we are just alike. Activities in this section help children to see how important it is that we are different and then to develop an appreciation for these differences and the people that bring them into our lives.

Something I Like About My Friend Who is Different ———— A Sharing Circle

Relates to: Language Arts (oral language) K-3

Objectives:

The children will demonstrate respect for and understanding of differences among people, cultures, lifestyles, attitudes, and abilities.

Note: This sharing circle may precede or follow the reading of Tomie dePaola's *Watch Out for Chicken Feet in Your Soup*, and corresponding activities.

Directions:

Review the sharing circle rules as necessary.

State the topic. Say to the children: *Today, we are going to talk about a friend who is different from us and what we like about him or her. The topic for this Sharing Circle is "Something I Like About My Friend Who Is Different."*

We are all alike and different in many ways. Today I want you to think about a friend who is different from you in at least one way— and why you like this person so much. Your friend might have a different size family than you, or be older than you. Does your friend speak a different language or eat different foods than you? Maybe your friend celebrates birthdays in a different way than you do, or has different holidays. What makes you like your friend so much? Does he or she play with you or share things with you? Invite you to birth-day celebrations? Sit down and read with you? Think about it for a few minutes. The topic is, "Something I Like About My Friend Who Is Different."

If necessary, give additional examples of differences in physical appearance, culture, or ability.

Involve the children in sharing.

Conduct a summary. When everyone who chooses to speak has done so, conduct a brief summary by asking open-ended questions, such as these:
— *In what ways are we different from our friends?*
— *Why do we like our friends even though they are different from us?*
— *Why is it helpful for us to remember what we like about our friends?*

Conclude the sharing circle.

Tasting Different Cultures —————

—————— *Reading, Discussion, and Experiencing*

Relates to: Social Studies and Language Arts (reading and speaking) K-3

Objectives: The children will demonstrate respect for and understanding of differences among people, cultures, lifestyles, attitudes, and abilities.

Time: approximately 1 to 1 1/2 hours

Materials Needed: a copy of Tomie dePaola's *Watch Out for Chicken Feet in Your Soup* (New York, Simon & Schuster, 1974), a large wall map of the world, tagboard sentence strips, paper plates and napkins, and plastic utensils

Directions: **Plan a cross-cultural food sampling day for the children.** Ask parents a week in advance if they will make simple ethnic foods that can be cut into bite-size pieces for the children to sample. Try to have a variety of cultures represented. Some examples might be lumpia (Philippines), guavas (Polynesian islands), scones and jam (England), roll tacos (Mexico), hummous and pita bread (Lebanon), or buñuelos (Columbia).

Read to the children dePaola's book *Watch Out for Chicken Feet in Your Soup.* It's about two young boys, Joey and Eugene, who go to visit Joey's Italian grandmother. She feeds them homemade chicken soup (complete with chicken feet) and spaghetti. She also invites Eugene to help her make bread dolls and sends the two boys off with their arms filled with freshly baked bread.

Discuss the story. After reading the story, talk about the soup with chicken feet. Ask the children if anyone has ever had soup like that. Use this example as a springboard to a discussion on foods that are popular with different ethnic groups. If you have

 (Continued Next Page)

pictures of foreign foods, show them to the children and ask if anyone has tried them. Tell the children that some of their parents have brought foods representing different cultures, and that they are going to have an opportunity to taste them.

Taste the foods. As the children sample each dish, write the name of the food on a strip of tagboard and pin it on a large wall map of the world, indicating where that kind of food originated. As the children are sampling the foods, ask them why they think it is important to try foods from different cultures. Discuss how it helps people understand and appreciate those who are different from them.

Conclude the activity. Let each child choose one of the foods tasted and draw a picture of it. Then have that child dictate a sentence describing his/her experience tasting that food. Write it below the picture. Post the pictures on the bulletin board.

Experiment with additional activities that teach about other cultures, such as breaking a piñata, doing a Chinese dragon dance, or making Japanese fish kites.

Extension: Another book that focuses on eating rituals in other cultures is *How My Parents Learned to Eat* by Ina Friedman, illustrated by Allan Say, Houghton Mifflin, 1984.

I Like Being Different —— *Art and Writing*

Relates to: Social Studies, Art, Math (sorting) and Language Arts (oral language and writing) K-3

Objectives:	The children will: —identify ways in which people are unique, as individuals. —demonstrate understanding and respect for differences among people, cultures, lifestyles, attitudes, and abilities.
Time:	two sessions, approximately 30 minutes each
Materials Needed:	a copy of the book, *Why Am I Different?* by Norma Simon, illustrated by Dora Leder (Chicago, Albert Whitman, 1979); large pieces of white butcher paper (one per student); pencils; tempera paints; scissors; and primary-level lined writing paper
Directions:	**Preparation:** Ask parent volunteers to come to class and help trace the outlines of the children on butcher paper, monitor the painting process, and write dictated descriptions on lined paper. If this is not possible, ask older students from other classes to help during the activity. **Introduce the activity:** Read Norma Simon's *Why Am I Different?* to the children. In this book, children see themselves as different in common areas such as physical growth, personal characteristics and conditions, abilities, family circumstances, cultural and religious background, occupation of parents, and more. The story emphasizes self-respect and respect for others while indicating that the children *like* being different. Tell the children that they are going to paint life-size images of themselves and then dictate some sentences that tell how they are different from others. Ask each child to lie down on a piece of butcher paper while the teacher or volunteer traces around his/her body with a pencil. Then have each child paint his/her image inside the traced outline. After the painted images are dry, allow the children (or older volunteers) to cut them out. Next have each child dictate to you or a volunteer the ways in which he or she is different from others. Write the sentences on the lined paper.

(Continued Next Page)

I Like Being Different ——————— *(Continued)*

Place each written piece next to its corresponding cut-out image and display the finished art all over the room. Have the children group or pattern the images, e.g., group by gender or hair color, or create a boy-girl-boy-girl pattern.

Conclusion: Read five or six of the dictated compositions each day until all of them have been read. After reading a piece, ask the author, "Do you like being different? Why do you think it is good to be different?" Reassure the children that our differences are a positive part of our world and make it more interesting.

What People Like About Me

A Sharing Circle

Relates to: Language Arts (oral language) K-3

Objectives: The children will describe positive characteristics about self as perceived by self and others.

Directions: **Review the sharing circle rules as necessary.**

State the topic. Say to the children: *Today our topic is, "What People Like About Me." Sometimes people tell us what they like about us. What have people told you? Maybe your family likes how helpful you are, or your friends tell you that you have a nice smile. Have people ever told you that they like the way you read or draw? Sometimes you can just tell what a person likes about you, without even being told. Maybe you know that you are appreciated as a friend or a thoughtful brother or sister. Take a few moments to think about it, and when you are ready, raise your hand. The topic is, "What People Like About Me."*

Involve the children in sharing.

Conduct a summary. Ask these and other questions to help generate a discussion of what was learned in the circle:
— *How does it feel to describe the things that others like about you?*
— *Why is it important to know that others recognize our positive qualities?*
— *Is it okay to ask people what they like best about us? Why or why not?*

Conclude the sharing circle.

Things I Like About You

A Special Group Session

Relates to: Language Arts (oral language) K-3

Objectives:

The children will:
—describe positive characteristics in others.
—demonstrate acceptance of the differences among people.

Time:

approximately 20 minutes

Directions:

Review the sharing circle rules. Although not a sharing circle, this special session will proceed more smoothly if you ask the children to follow the circle rules. Have the children sit in a circle, and review each rule with them.

Explain the procedure. Say to the children: *During this special sharing session, we are going to take turns telling others what we like about them. When it is your turn, look at each member of the circle in turn, and tell that person the most positive thing we can think of about him or her. Maybe you like the way the person includes you in games. Perhaps you like the person's hair or clothes. Or maybe you like the way he or she says hello to you each day. Everyone in this circle has many positive characteristics, and now is our opportunity to recognize some of them. When you receive a compliment, simply say, "thank you." This is not a time for conversation, but rather, a chance to tell others what we like about them.*

Take you turn first and model the procedure. Compliment one of the children and wait for the child to say thank you. Then say something positive about another child, and so on, allowing time for each child to respond. You may choose randomly or move systematically around the circle, whichever is more comfortable.

Conclude the special session. Thank the children for making this such an enjoyable and special time together.

An Activity My Family Enjoys Together
——————— A Sharing Circle

Relates to: Language Arts (oral language) 4-6

Objectives:

The children will:
— describe leisure activities pursued by self and family.
— identify differences among activities persued by self and others.

Directions:

Review the sharing circle rules as necessary.

State the topic. Say to the children: *Today's topic is, "An Activity My Family Enjoys Together." There are lots of things families enjoy doing together. Some involve work and others are strictly play. Maybe your family enjoys camping or driving off-road vehicles. Perhaps your family holds big celebrations on special occasions like birthdays and holidays. Or maybe you always go to Sunday brunch together. During the summer, you may have picnics at the beach, or in the winter, head for the ski slopes. Does your family read together, participate in crafts, or operate a family booth at swap meets? Take a few moments to think of something your family enjoys doing together, and raise your hand when you are ready to share. The topic is, "An Activity My Family Enjoys Together."*

Involve the children in sharing.

Conduct a summary. Invite the children to talk about what they learned in the circle. Ask these and other questions to generate a discussion:
— *How do family activities make our lives happier?*
— *Do all families have the time to share activities together? Why or why not?*
— *What differences did you notice among the activities we enjoy with our families?*

Conclude the sharing circle.

An Activity I Enjoy When I'm by Myself ——————— A Sharing Circle

Relates to: Language Arts (oral language) 4-6

Objectives:

The children will:
— describe leisure activities pursued alone.
— identify differences among activities pursued by self and peers.

Directions:

Review the sharing circle rules as necessary.

State the topic. Say to the children: *In previous sessions, we've talked about activities we enjoy doing with friends and family. Now we're going to discuss things we do when we're alone. The topic is, "An Activity I Enjoy When I'm by Myself."*

What do you like to do when you're alone? Maybe you enjoy reading or putting puzzles together. Possibly you like to build elaborate constructions or perfect your video-game skills. Maybe you enjoy imagining things or listening to music. Do you write stories or poems, draw pictures, or perform science experiments? Maybe you prefer to be outdoors, riding your skateboard or bicycle, or daydreaming quietly while relaxing in a special place. Think about it for a few moments. Raise your hand to show that you are ready. The topic is, "An Activity I Enjoy When I'm by Myself."

Involve the children in sharing.

Conduct a summary. Invite the children to discuss what they learned in the circle. Ask several open-ended questions, such as these:
— *How do the activities we enjoy differ?*
— *Do you think you will still enjoy your activity as an adult? Why or why not?*
— *How do you feel when you are involved in your activity?*
— *How do you feel about being alone?*
— *What are some things that you can do alone that are difficult to do when other people are around?*

Conclude the sharing circle.

An Activity I Enjoy with Friends

A Sharing Circle

Relates to: Language Arts (oral language) 4-6

Objectives:
The children will:
—describe leisure activities pursued by self and friends.
—identify differences among activities pursued by self and those pursued by peers.

Directions:
Review the sharing circle rules as necessary.

State the topic. In your own words, say to the children: *Today's topic is, "An Activity I Enjoy with Friends." We all enjoy doing things with our friends. What do you particularly like to do? Maybe you enjoy playing a sport or working on model planes or cars. Perhaps you like to go to the shopping mall with your friends, or watch television. Do you and your friends play video games, or go bicycling or skating? Do you build things out of odds and ends, LEGOS, building blocks, or logs? Do you make up plays and act in them? Whatever it is you most enjoy doing with your friends, please tell us about it. I'll give you a few moments to decide. When you are ready, raise your hand. The topic is, "An Activity I Enjoy Doing with Friends."*

Involve the children in sharing.

Conduct a summary. Give the children an opportunity to talk about what they learned in the circle. Use these and other open-ended questions to generate discussion:
—*What kinds of things did most of us enjoy doing with our friends?*
—*Why do we often do different things with different friends?*
—*Who usually decides what you and your friends are going to do? What do you do when you disagree?*
—*Do you think any of the things you do with your friends could develop into careers? Which ones?*

Conclude the sharing circle.

RESOLVING CONFLICTS

The ability to manage conflicts is an important life skill. Interpersonal conflict is an inevitable part of life and cannot be entirely avoided, nor should it be in some cases. Therefore, the activities in this section help students to understand the dynamics of conflict and to manage conflicts without jeopardizing self-esteem.

Why We Have Rules — *Discussion and Art*

Relates to: Social Studies, Language Arts (oral language), and Art, K-3

Objectives: The children will demonstrate skills in resolving conflicts with peers and adults.

Time: approximately 45 minutes

Materials Needed: construction paper and crayons

Directions: **Introduce the activity.** Discuss with the children the fact that we all have to follow rules. For example, adults have rules in their workplaces and on the road, and children have rules at home and at school. Ask the children to describe some of the rules they have in their families. Write the rules on the chalkboard and point out similarities and differences. Next, ask the children to watch each other during playtime, and to be ready for a class discussion afterwards.

Lead a discussion. After playtime, generate a discussion concerning situations on the playground in which the existence of rules would help avoid problems. Let the children tell about real or potential conflicts during playtime. Talk about any existing school rules, such as taking turns on the equipment or getting in line to climb the slide ladder. List these rules on the chalkboard. Ask volunteers to act out situations that could occur if there were no rules and then reenact them, applying the rules. Explain that rules are made to prevent problems and conflicts.

Ask the children to each draw a picture illustrating one of the rules that helps prevent conflict in school. Have each child dictate to you the rule that applies to his/her drawing. Write it directly on the drawing. Display the illustrated rules around the room.

Conclusion: Ask the children, *Why is it important to remember and follow rules?* Thank them for following the school rules so well.

Ways to Solve Problems ──────

────── *Discussion and Drama*

Relates to: Social Studies, Language Arts, and Math (sorting) K-3

Objectives: The children will demonstrate skills in resolving conflicts with peers and adults.

Note: This activity coordinates with, "Why We Have Rules." Both treat the subject of conflict management. This activity addresses the concept of resolving conflicts, and the next one deals with preventing conflicts.

Time: approximately 20 minutes

Materials Needed: chalkboard and chalk

Directions: **Introduce the activity.** Say: *I am going to tell you about some problem situations and I want you to help me solve them. They are small problems that you might come across in the classroom someday, and if you can think about how to solve them ahead of time, they might not become big problems.*

Give an example of a conflict that might arise in the class, and ask the children to think of a good way to resolve it. Say, for example: *Jimmy and Brittany both want to use the red paint, but only one can use it at a time. They both grab the brush and start pulling on it. What should they do?*

Give the children a few moments to think about possible resolutions, and then ask for responses. Write their suggestions on the board. List all possible solutions. Read back the suggestions and have the children sort them into two groups, "possible" and "impossible." Then ask them to decide which one would work best. (A solution would be to take turns.) If you think that their choices are unwise, ask why they would not work. Continue this way through several examples.

(Continued Next Page)

Ways to Solve Problems ———— *(Continued)*

Conflict situations and possible solutions:

- Marla thinks that Danny has taken her red crayon so she yells at him and hits him. Then she finds her crayon under her paper. What should she do? (Say, "I'm sorry.")
- Peter has accidently bumped into Jennifer and made her drop all of the crackers on the floor. What should he do? (Say, "I'm sorry," and help her pick them up.)
- Tammy and Michael are playing house and Charlene asks if she can play, too. Tammy says, "No." What should Michael do? (Tell Tammy that he would like to include Charlene.)
- Everyone sits down with a book to read except Tyrone, who forgot to bring his book. He taps his foot loudly because he has nothing to do. What would you do if you were sitting next to him? (Share your book with him.)
- Diane is having trouble writing her name. She gets angry and scribbles on Yvette's paper. What should she do instead? (Ask for help.)

After you and the children have chosen the best solution for each conflict, ask volunteers to act them out, one at a time.

Conclusion: Ask the children these and other questions:
— *Why do you think it is helpful for us to talk about and practice pretend problems and how to resolve them?*
— *How do you feel about being able to solve problems?*

Emotional Chain Reactions ————

—— Two Chain-Writing Activities and Discussion

Relates to: Drama and Language Arts (oral language) K-3

Objectives:

The children will describe how one person's behavior can influence the feelings and actions of others.

Note: This is the first of three activities having to do with emotional "chain reactions." In it, the children demonstrate how feelings and behaviors—both negative and positive—tend to perpetuate themselves.

Time:

approximately 30 minutes

Materials Needed:

magic marker and two large sheets of lined chart paper

Directions:

Preparation: On chart #1, write: *Johnny was walking home from school when Tom, a sixth grader, ran into him and knocked him over. Johnny...*

On chart #2, write: *Johnny was on his way to school when Tom, a sixth grader, came up to him and said, "Hi Johnny. How's it going?" Johnny...*

Introduce the activity. Ask the children: *Do you know what a chain reaction is?* Discuss examples. For instance, tell the children: *It's a windy day. The wind blows through a window in your house. It knocks down a lamp. The lamp falls on your cat, who runs for the door. You come running in with a broom. The cat hits the broom and knocks it out of your hand. The handle falls on one of your bare feet. You hop around holding your foot, and your brother sees you and says, "is that a new dance?"* This example of a chain reaction shows how the wind caused your brother to think you were practicing a new dance.

(Continued Next Page)

Emotional Chain Reactions — *(Continued)*

Elaborate. *There are emotional chain reactions too. For example, something happens that makes Maria mad. That causes Maria to do something that Tom doesn't like, and he feels bad. So Tom reacts by doing something to Jerry and Jerry gets mad at Chris—and so on. Have you ever had someone treat you badly and then found out that the person did it because he or she was treated badly beforehand? And then, after you were treated badly, you felt like treating someone else badly too?*

Explain the activity. Hold up chart #1, read it with the children, and suggest that they help you write a chain-reaction story. Ask: *What should we have Johnny do?* Help the children put the next part of the story into words. As they dictate, write their suggestions on the chart. For example, the story could continue with Johnny being rude or hurtful to a second person, and that person doing something to a third person, and so on, until six or seven people have treated other people badly because they were treated badly.

Read the finished story aloud to the children, while they read it to themselves. Then read it in unison.

Next, ask the children: *Are all emotional chain reactions bad ones? Is it possible for one person to treat another person kindly and respectfully, and that person, feeling good, to do the same thing to someone else, who in turn, does the same thing to yet another person? Have you ever had someone treat you so well that you just couldn't help but be nice to the next person you talked to?*

Hold up chart #2, and ask the children to help you create a positive chain-reaction story. Make sure that the second story is as long and well thought out as the first. After it is complete, read the story aloud to the children, while they read it to themselves. Then read it in unison.

 (Continued Next Page)

Emotional Chain Reactions — *(Continued)*

Lead a summary discussion. Here are some questions to ask the children:
— *Why do we do something mean to another person after some-one else has been mean to us?*
— *If someone is mean to you, do you <u>have</u> to be mean to someone else?*
— *How can you stop a bad chain reaction?*
— *What makes a good chain reaction work?*

Discuss the feeling of wanting to "get even." Explain that it is a normal human urge, and while the feeling itself is not bad, acting on the feeling in a way that hurts an innocent person, is bad. Suggest that bad emotional chain reactions keep going because the people involved don't think about what they are doing, or stop themselves from acting badly toward innocent people.

Good chain reactions work because "courtesy is contagious." It is fun to start *good* chain reactions and keep them going.

Conclude the activity. Thank the children for doing such a fine job of thinking, speaking, and listening.

Illustrating the "Chain-Reaction Stories" ——— Art, Reading, and Discussion

Relates to: Art and Language Arts (reading and oral language) K-3

Objectives:

The children will:
— describe how one person's behavior can influence the feelings and actions of others.
— describe how negative chain-reaction situations contribute to conflict.

Note: This is the second in a sequence of three activities having to do with emotional "chain reactions."

Time:

approximately 40 minutes for assigning and making illustrations, approximately 20 to 30 minutes for viewing and reading the completed stories

Materials Needed:

the two charts from the previous activity, sturdy art paper in pastel colors (at least 8 1/2 inches by 11 inches in size), and crayons

Directions:

Introduce and organize the activity. With the two "chain-reaction stories" from the previous activity close at hand, suggest to the children: *We did such a good job writing these stories. Now let's illustrate them. There are lots of different scenes. Let's decide who will draw a picture for each one.*

Read the first line of the first story. Then, have the children read it with you in unison. Finally, ask: *What should the picture for this part of the story look like?* Listen to and validate any suggestions the children make. Then, choose a volunteer to complete the illustration. Continue in this manner until each page has been read, ideas for an illustration have been discussed, and an illustrator has been assigned. (Jot down who is illustrating each page in order to make reminders and avoid mix-ups later.)

If some children fail to get an assignment, tell them that their pictures will be used to illustrate posters "advertising" the story. By this time the children will probably be eager to start.

(Continued Next Page)

Illustrating the "Chain-Reaction Stories"

(Continued)

As the children work, assist them with their illustrations only as absolutely necessary. Encourage them to make their illustrations large. Talk with the children individually about their drawings, making many positive comments. Encourage those who can write to make cartoon bubbles containing the words that the various characters say.

Place and secure the finished illustrations in sequential order, along with the appropriate chain-reaction story, on a wall or bulletin board.

View the illustrations. After the drawings have been posted, admire them with the children. Give each illustrator credit for his or her art work. Read the first chain-reaction story to the children while they read along silently. Then ask them to read it with you in unison. Do the same with the second chain-reaction story.

Conclude the activity. Thank the children for drawing such fine illustrations for their chain-reaction stories.

"Chain Reaction" Theater

Drama and Discussion

Relates to: Drama and Language Arts (oral language) K-3

Objectives: The children will describe how one person's behavior can influence the feelings and actions of others.

Note: This is the third of three activities having to do with emotional "chain reactions." By role-playing the stories they created in the two previous activities, the children demonstrate their understanding of how one person's behavior can influence the feelings and actions of others.

Time: approximately 40 minutes

Directions: **Introduce the activity:** In your own words, suggest to the children: *We've been having a lot of fun writing chain-reaction stories and illustrating them. We've also been learning about how "emotional chain reactions" work. Today, let's learn more about emotional chain reactions by dramatizing the two stories we wrote. We'll start with our first story, which was about a bad chain reaction. Let's assign parts. We need someone to play the parts of Johnny and Tom, the sixth grader...*

Continue assigning roles until all of them are taken. Involve as many of the children as possible.

Dramatize the first story. Direct and guide the children through an extemporaneous dramatization of their first chain-reaction story. At the end of the dramatization, have each player take a bow, and lead the group in applause. Then ask the children:
—*Tom started this bad chain reaction. What do you think might have happened to him to cause him to start it?*
—*If someone treats you badly—like Tom treated Johnny—what can you do?*
—*What will you try to remember not to do?*

(Continued Next Page)

"Chain Reaction" Theater

Set up and dramatize the second chain-reaction story. As with the first story, assign roles and guide the players through the dramatization. Be sure to involve children who did not participate in the first dramatization. After final bows and audience applause, ask the group:

— *This story started with Tom being friendly to Johnny. Why do you think he was friendly?*

— *Can you start a good chain reaction? Can you keep one going?*

— *What have we learned about emotional chain reactions?*

Discuss the fact that good feelings are just as likely to be passed on from one person to another as are bad feelings—and that anyone can start (and perpetuate) a good chain reaction just by being friendly and respectful to others.

Conclusion: Thank the children for doing such a fine job of acting, thinking, speaking, and listening.

I Almost Got Into a Fight

A Sharing Circle

Relates to: Language Arts (oral language) K-3

Objectives: The children will demonstrate skills in resolving conflicts with peers and adults.

Directions: **Review the sharing circle rules as necessary.**

State the topic. Say: *Today we are going to talk about a time when you were so angry with another person that you almost got into a fight. In fact, today's topic is exactly that: "I Almost Got Into a Fight."*

Explain to the children: *Each of us has been angry or upset at another person. Sometimes we disagree about something. Other times we are hurt about the way the person has treated us or someone we like. Or the other person thinks that <u>we</u> have done something to hurt <u>him</u> or <u>her</u>. Think of a time when something happened between you and another person that almost caused you to get into a fight. Maybe you were the one who wanted to fight because you were so mad, or perhaps the other person tried to start the fight. Perhaps you both felt like fighting, but you decided not to and tried to get over your angry feelings. Tell us how this happened. Don't mention anyone's name, just say what happened that made you almost start fighting. Close your eyes and think quietly about it. When you look up at me, I'll know that you are ready to begin the circle. Once again, the topic is, "I Almost Got Into a Fight."*

Involve the children in sharing.

Conduct a summary. When every child has had a turn to speak, ask the children some open-ended questions to encourage critical thinking:
— *How can conflict, or disagreement, lead to <u>good</u> feelings?*
— *What are some ways in which we can keep from getting into a fight, even if we feel like fighting?*
— *Why do you think it is better to figure out solutions to problems than to fight about them?*

Conclude the sharing circle.

178

Managing Stress and Conflict

Role Playing and Discussion

Relates to: Social Studies and Language Arts (oral language) K-3

Objectives:

The children will:
— describe and discuss causes of stress and conflict.
— demonstrate ways of dealing with reactions of others under stress and conflict.
— demonstrate healthful ways of coping with conflicts, stress, and emotions.

Time: approximately 30 minutes

Directions:

Introduce the activity. Talk to the children about ways in which situations that might cause a fight between two or more people can be resolved. Suggest the following ideas:
• They can share or take turns.
• One person can stop arguing and listen carefully to the other.
• One person can say that he or she is sorry.
• Both people can decide to compromise—have (or do) a little of what each person wants.

Next, ask the children to help you think of situations in which there could be a potential fight among children. Allow the children to contribute their ideas and list them in a column on the chalkboard. After you get five or six ideas, ask the children to suggest healthful ways of dealing with each situation. List the ideas next to the conflict situation.

Invite volunteers to act out at least one resolution to each situation. After each role play, ask the class a few open-ended questions such as these:
— *Why do you think that this solution would or would not solve the problem?*
— *Are there other ways that a person could handle the situation?*
— *Why is it helpful to talk about and act out these situations, even if they haven't happened yet?*
— *How can learning to solve this type of problem here at school help when you grow up and have a job?*

 (Continued Next Page)

Use these additional situations, if you would like more:

• At recess, three children are bouncing the ball to each other, but one is throwing it too hard, making the other two miss. The other two are getting angry. What can they do to resolve the situation?

• Three children are at home watching television. Each one wants to watch a different program and they are arguing over who will get his or her way. How can they solve the problem?

• Two children are sitting at their desks at school. One forgot to do her homework. She wants to get it done before school starts and the teacher checks for it. The second student wants to talk about an upcoming birthday party and who will be invited. The first student snaps at the second to be quiet and the second doesn't understand what she did wrong. What can both children do?

• A child comes to school the day after his pet parakeet has died. He is upset, but won't tell anyone because he is afraid he might cry. His friend asks to borrow his colored markers and he shouts, "No, you always lose one!" The friend knows that he has never lost one and starts to shout back. What can they do?

Conclude the activity. Conduct a review of the ways in which children can resolve conflicts and cope with negative emotions. Thank them for their excellent ideas and active participation.

Two Sides of the Same Story

Literature and Discussion

Relates to: Language Arts (listening, speaking, reading, and writing) K-3

Objectives:

The children will:
—identify different views of the same incident and describe how those can lead to conflict.
—identify strategies for resolving conflict.

Time:

approximately 45 minutes

Materials Needed:

a traditional version of the tale *The Three Little Pigs*, such as the one by James Marshall, New York, Dial Press, 1989, or the one by William Pene du Bois, New York, Viking Press, 1962; and a copy of the book *The True Story of the Three Little Pigs*, by Jon Scieszka, New York, Viking Kestrel, 1989

Directions:

Introduce the activity. Explain to the children that every argument has two sides. Stress that it is important to try to understand the other person's view in order to resolve some conflicts and prevent possible fights. Say that you are going to read them two versions of the familiar tale, *The Three Little Pigs*. Ask the children to listen carefully to both sides of this story.

Read both of the books to the children. *The Three Little Pigs* is the familiar tale in which only one of three brother pigs survives a wolf's huffing and puffing attacks. *The True Story of the Three Little Pigs* is the wolf's version of what happened when he encountered the three little pigs. According to the wolf, he was merely going from house to house to borrow a cup of sugar so he could make a birthday cake for his dear old granny. Since he had a terrible cold, he sneezed a big sneeze at each house, knocking down the straw and stick houses which, in turn, killed the first two pigs. Rather than let the lovely "hams" just spoil, he had to eat them. At the brick house, he was insulted by the third pig and apprehended by the police.

            (Continued Next Page)

Draw a vertical line down the center of the chalkboard to make a chart. Write "Pig's Perspective" at the top of one side and "Wolf's Perspective" at the top of the other side. Explain that a *perspective* is someone's point of view or opinion. Have the children list the sequence of events in the two stories: first, from the pigs' perspective and second, from the wolf's perspective.

After making the two lists, lead a discussion by asking some open-ended questions, such as the following:
— *Why is it important to look at both viewpoints in an argument or situation?*
— *If we disagree with a person, what are some of the things we can do to try to understand his or her perspective?*

Conclude the activity. Thank the children for being such good thinkers. Encourage them to look at all perspectives of an event before expressing an opinion.

Extension: Role-play this story from both perspectives or have the children rewrite another fairy tale from the viewpoint of the villain.

The Other Side of the Story

Listening, Writing, and Discussion

Relates to: **Language Arts (literature, writing, and oral language) 4-6**

Objectives: The children will:
—describe how one's behavior influences the feelings and actions of others.
—describe and discuss causes of stress and conflict.
—describe healthful ways of coping with conflicts, stress, and emotions.

Time: approximately 15 to 20 minutes

Materials Needed: a copy of "The Maligned Wolf" (provided)

Directions: **Introduce the activity.** Gather the children together and tell them that you have a story to read to them, called "The Maligned Wolf."

Begin reading the story. Very quickly, the children will recognize the story as *Little Red Riding Hood*, told from the point of view of the wolf. Expect excitement and keen interest at this point.

Lead a discussion. Here are some questions to ask the children after you have finished reading the story. Accept responses from all children who volunteer.
—*Have you heard this story before? What was different about this version?*
—*Why does everyone have a right to his or her own point of view?*
—*What does this story teach us about conflicts?*
—*What are some other stories that can be retold from the point of view of the villain? What about Jack and the Beanstalk? What would the giant say if we considered the story from his point of view?*

Conclude the activity. Point out that the children can help prevent or resolve conflict by considering things from the point of view of the other person. Thank the children for listening and participating.

 (Continued Next Page)

The Maligned Wolf

By Leif Fearn

The forest was my home. I lived there and I cared about it. I tried to keep it neat and clean.

Then one sunny day, while I was cleaning up some garbage a camper had left behind, I heard footsteps. I leaped behind a tree and saw a rather plain little girl coming down the trail carrying a basket. I was suspicious of this little girl right away because she was dressed funny—all in red, and her head covered up so it seemed like she didn't want people to know who she was. Naturally, I stopped to check her out. I asked who she was, where she was going, where she had come from, and all that.

She gave me a song and dance about going to her grandmother's house with a basket of lunch. She appeared to be a basically honest person, but she was in my forest and she certainly looked suspicious with that strange getup of hers. So I decided to teach her just how serious it is to prance through the forest unannounced and dressed funny.

I let her go on her way, but I ran ahead to her grandmother's house. When I saw that nice old woman, I explained my problem and she agreed that her granddaughter needed to learn a lesson, all right. The old woman agreed to stay out of sight until I called her. Actually, she hid under the bed.

When the girl arrived, I invited her into the bedroom where I was in the bed, dressed like the grandmother. The girl came in all rosy-cheeked and said something nasty about my big ears. I've been insulted before so I made the best of it by suggesting that my big ears would help me to hear better. Now, what I meant was that I liked her and wanted to pay close attention to what she was saying. But she makes another insulting crack about my bulging eyes. Now you can see how I was beginning to feel about this girl who put on such a nice front, but was apparently a very nasty person. Still, I've made it a policy to try to ignore put-downs, so I told her that my big eyes helped me to see her better.

Her next insult really got to me. I've got this problem with having big teeth. And that little girl made an insulting crack about them. I know that I should have had better control, but I leaped up from that bed and growled that my teeth would help me to eat her better.

Now let's face it—no wolf has ever eaten a little girl—everyone knows that. But that crazy girl started running around the house screaming with me chasing her trying to calm her down. I'd taken off the grandmother clothes, but that only seemed to make things worse.

All of a sudden the door came crashing open and a big lumberjack was standing here with his axe. I looked at him and all of a sudden it became clear that I was in deep trouble. There was an open window behind me and out I went.

I'd like to say that was the end of it. But that grandmother character never did tell my side of the story. Before long the word got around that I was a terrible, mean guy. Everybody started shooting at me. I don't know about that little girl with the funny red outfit, but *I* didn't live happily ever after. In fact, now us wolves are an endangered specie. And I'm sure that little girl's story has had a lot to do with it!

Conflict Management Strategies ———
——— Experience Sheet, Drama, and Discussion

Relates to: **Language Arts (reading and oral language) and Drama, 4-6**

Objectives: The children will:
— describe how one's behavior influences the feelings and actions of others.
— demonstrate skills in resolving conflicts with peers and adults.
— describe and discuss causes of stress and conflict.
— demonstrate ways of dealing with reactions of others under stress and conflict.

Time: approximately 10 to 15 minutes to read and discuss each conflict management strategy (may be done in several sessions)

Materials Needed: a pencil and one copy of the experience sheet, "Conflict Management Strategies" for each child

Directions: **Distribute the experience sheets to the children.** Write the words *conflict management* on the chalkboard. Define both words separately; then define the term. Ask:
— *How many of you have ever been in a conflict that was really terrible, where you or someone else got hurt physically, or had your feelings hurt badly?*
— *Have you ever been in a conflict that worked out well for everyone?*

Ask a few of the children who respond affirmatively to the second question to describe those conflicts. Then analyze them briefly. Point out instances in which the people involved used strategies or behaviors similar to those described in the experience sheet. Emphasize that by using these strategies, they showed respect for each other—and for themselves.

 (Continued Next Page)

Conflict Management Strategies —

Read each strategy aloud to the children while they read along silently. Write the strategy on the chalkboard and define it. Discuss the strategy with the children—then give them opportunities to practice it. Here are some suggestions:

• **Active listening:** Ask volunteers to practice making statements (those listed on the experience sheet and others) that indicate they are listening.

• **"I" messages:** Think of several conflict situations and ask volunteers to role play them. Help the actors formulate first "you" messages (blaming, name-calling) and then "I" messages (stating feelings, perceptions). Discuss the differences.

• **Compromise:** Brainstorm a list of compromise statements like those listed in the experience sheet. Practice saying some of them.

• **Taking turns:** Describe a familiar conflict situation to the children, e.g., *two students want to use the class computer at the same time.* Allow volunteers to demonstrate different ways of "taking turns," such as flipping a coin, drawing straws, and choosing a number between one and ten.

• **Putting it off:** Let several children practice making statements that suggest putting off the resolution of the conflict until a later time. Discuss the importance of keeping the commitment to return to the conflict, rather than just forgetting about it.

• **Getting help:** Ask the children to remember times when they used this strategy. Discuss one or two examples.

• **Expressing regret:** The difference between apologizing and expressing regret is subtle even for adults, so spend some time discussing this one. Then let the children practice making the statements shown on the experience sheet.

Discuss unacceptable and "last resort" responses to conflict. List the words *violence, tattling,* and *running away* on the chalkboard. Discuss each one. Here are some suggestions for things you might say:

Violence: If someone becomes violent with you, you must either leave the situation or defend yourself. However, violence usually destroys any possibility of settling the conflict so that both people are satisfied. By the way, saying cruel things to another person is a form of violence.

186   **(Continued Next Page)**

Tattling: When you tell on someone, it is usually because you want to get the person in trouble. Tattling never helps settle conflicts; it only makes the other person mad. So, instead of tattling, manage your own conflicts. If you decide to ask for help, remember that the help is for both you and the other person in the conflict.

Running away: If you are about to get hurt, leave the situation as fast as you can. But don't get in the habit of running away from conflict. Respect yourself and the other person enough to stay and try to settle the conflict. Say how you feel and what you think. Listen. Use the conflict management strategies.

Conclude the activity. Thank the children for their active participation.

Conflict Management Strategies

Have you ever been in a conflict? Of course!
Some conflicts are terrible experiences that cause hurt feelings and even hurt bodies. Other conflicts aren't so bad. Some can even lead to good things. How does that happen? How can you make a conflict turn out well? By *managing* the conflict. Here are some ways to do it:

Listen—*actively!*
Often people get into conflicts because they don't really listen to each other or they misunderstand what they hear. So try *really* listening to the other person's point of view. Tune in to the words—and the feelings too. To let the other person know that you are listening, say things like:

"Okay, I'm listening."

"Go ahead. You talk first and I'll listen."

"Let me see if I heard you right. You said..."

Use "I" messages.
Show the other person that you are willing to take responsibility for your feelings and the way you view the conflict. Don't use name-calling, blaming "you" messages, like:

"Hey stupid, you hogged all the milk again!"

Instead, say what you think and how you feel, with an "I" message, like:

"I'm thirsty. I feel bad when there's no milk left for me."

Try to compromise.
If you are willing to give up a little of what you want, and the other person is too, then you can both have at least *part* of what you want. That's a *compromise.* You compromise when you make suggestions like these:

"I'll take half and you take half."

"I'll go to the park with you in the morning, if you'll go to the mall with me in the afternoon."

"I'll mow the lawn, and you sweep the walks."

          (Continued Next Page)

Take turns.

Some conflicts happen because two people want the same thing at the same time. Show the other person that you are willing to be *second* sometimes. Flip a coin, draw straws, guess a number between one and ten, or say:

"You go first because I'm bigger."

Put it off.

If you are mad, tired, hungry, or in a hurry—or if you think the other person is—wait! Put off dealing with the conflict until later. Say:

"I want to settle this, but now's not the time. What about waiting until after lunch?"

"Everything seems to be going wrong. I'm too tired to think straight. Could we get back to this later?"

Get help.

Bring someone into the conflict who can help settle it. This may sound like tattling, but it's not. Tattling is trying to get the other person in trouble; getting help is asking another person to help straighten things out. For example, if you and a friend disagree about how a word should be pronounced, ask your teacher.

Express regret.

Let the other person know that you are sorry the conflict happened. You *don't* have to admit you are wrong or that the conflict is your fault. Just say:

"It's too bad this happened."

"I know you're upset and I feel bad about it."

I Got Into a Conflict

A Sharing Circle

Relates to: Language Arts (oral language) 4-6

Objectives:

The children will:
— describe how one's behavior influences the feelings and actions of others.
— describe and discuss causes of stress and conflict.
— describe ways of dealing with reactions of others under stress and conflict.
— describe healthful ways of coping with conflicts, stress, and emotions.

Materials Needed:

paper and pencil for note-taking (teacher only)

Directions:

Review the sharing circle rules as necessary.

State the topic: Say to the children: *Our topic today is, "I Got Into a Conflict." Conflicts are very common. They occur because of big and little things that happen in our lives. And sometimes the littlest things that happen can lead to the biggest conflicts. This is your opportunity to talk about a time when you had an argument or fight with someone. Maybe you and a friend argued over something that one of you said that the other didn't like. Or maybe you argued with a brother or sister over what TV show to watch, or who should do a particular chore around the house. Have you ever had a fight because someone broke a promise or couldn't keep a secret? If you feel comfortable telling us what happened, we'd like to hear it. Describe what the other person did and said, and what you did and said. Tell us how you felt and how the other person seemed to feel. There's just one thing you shouldn't tell us and that's the name of the other person, OK? Take a few moments to think about it. When you are ready, raise your hand. The topic is, "I Got Into a Conflict."*

(Continued Next Page)

I Got Into a Conflict

Involve the children in sharing.

Note: Jot down a brief description of each conflict situation shared for use in the next activity.

Conduct a summary. Ask these and other questions to help generate a free-flowing discussion:
— *How did most of us feel when we were part of a conflict?*
— *What kinds of things led to the conflicts that we shared?*
— *How could some of our conflicts have been prevented?*
— *What conflict management strategies could have been used in the situations that we shared? Be specific.*

Conclude the sharing circle. Tell the children that in the next activity, they will have an opportunity to act out some of the conflict episodes described in this session—first the way they actually happened, and then using a conflict management strategy. Thank the children for sharing their experiences and for listening so well during this sharing circle.

Demonstrating Conflict Management Strategies —— Role Play and Discussion

Relates to: Drama and Language Arts (oral language) 4-6

Objectives:

The children will:
— describe how one's behavior influences the feelings and actions of others.
— demonstrate skills in resolving conflicts with peers and adults.
— describe and discuss causes of stress and conflict.
— demonstrate ways of dealing with reactions of others under stress and conflict.

Note: In this activity, the children dramatize events disclosed in the sharing circle, "I Got Into a Conflict," and apply techniques presented in the experience sheet, "Conflict Management Strategies." Both are prerequisite activities.

Time: approximately 40 minutes

Materials Needed: a list of the conflict situations discussed during the last sharing circle; a list of the conflict management strategies on chart paper, or a copy of the experience sheet, "Conflict Management Strategies" for each child

Directions: **Introduce the activity.** In your own words suggest to the children: *In our last sharing circle, we told one another about times we got into conflicts. Now let's act out some of the episodes we shared. If your episode is chosen, you will be the director. You can ask other "actors" to help you. Tell them what to say and do to make the event exactly like it was when it actually happened. Afterwards, the rest of us will suggest conflict management strategies that you can use to make the situation better. Pick one strategy and act out the situation again, using that strategy. The person who suggested the strategy will be your director for the second role play.*

(Continued Next Page)

Demonstrating Conflict Management Strategies ——————————— (Continued)

Begin the dramatizations. Select a child whose conflict situation will lend itself well to role playing, and ask the child to direct and "star" in his or her own scenario. Assist with the selection and coaching of supporting actors. Then watch with the other children as the conflict scenario is recreated. Afterwards, ask the group: *Which conflict management strategies could be used in this scenario? Which strategies might help settle this argument (fight)?*

Call on several children and hear their ideas. Jot down all ideas on the chalkboard or chart paper. Then ask the "star" to choose one strategy and act it out, with the child who made the suggestion serving as the new director.

Debrief each scenario. Immediately after each set of dramatizations, ask these and other questions to help the children evaluate the results of their use of conflict management strategies:
— *How did you (the actors) feel, using the conflict management strategy?*
— *How do you (the actors) think it worked?*
— *How does the group think it worked?*
— *How many of you will try using this conflict management strategy to settle a real conflict?*

Select a second conflict situation and repeat the process. Continue with the dramatizations as long as the children remain interested.

Conduct a summary discussion. Give all of the children an opportunity to respond to this summarizing question:
— *What is the most important thing you have learned about conflict from this activity and the other conflict-management activities we have done?*

Conclude the activity. Thank the children for the fine acting, thinking, speaking and listening they demonstrated during this activity.

Resources

Armstrong, Thomas, Ph.D. *In Their Own Way,* Los Angeles:
    J.P. Tarcher, Inc., 1987.

Ball, Geraldine, Ph.D. *The Magic Circle - Human
    Development Program, Pre-Kindergarten - Level VI*, San
    Clemente, California: Magic Circle Publishing, 1974.

Bloomfield, Harold H. *Making Peace With Your Parents*, New
    York: Random House, 1983.

Bluestein, Jane, Ph.D. *21st Century Discipline*, Instructor Books,
    1988.

Bluestein, Jane, Ph.D. *Being a Successful Teacher*, Belmont,
    California: Fearon Teacher Aids, 1989.

Borba, Michele. *Esteem Builders*, Rolling Hills Estates,
    California: Jalmar Press, 1989.

Branden, Nathaniel. *The Psychology of Self Esteem*, New York:
    Bantam Books, 1971.

Briggs, Dorothy Corkille Briggs. *Your Child's Self-Esteem*,
    Garden City, NY: Doubleday, 1970.

Brown, George I. *Human Teaching for Human Learning: An
    Introduction to Confluent Education*, New York: Viking Press,
    1971

Buscaglia, Leo. *Love*, Greenwich, CT: Fawcett Books, 1972.

Buscaglia, Leo. *Living, Loving & Learning*, Thorofare, NJ:
    Charles B. Slack, Inc., 1982.

Chase, Larry. *The Other Side of the Report Card*, Santa Monica,
    CA: Goodyear Publishing Co., 1975.

Clark, Barbara, Ph.D. *Optimizing Learning*, Columbus, Ohio:
    Merrill Publishing Co.,1986.

Davis, Robbins, McKay, and Eshelman. *The Relaxation & Stress
    Reduction Workbook*, Oakland,California: New Harbinger
    Publications, 1988.

Fanning, Patrick. *Visualization for Change*, Oakland, California:
    New Harbinger Publications, Inc., 1988.

Fluegelman, Andrew. *The New Games Book*, New York:
    Doubleday/Dolphin, 1976.

Resources (Continued)

Frey, Diane, Ph.D. and Carlock, Jesse C., Ph.D. *Enhancing Self Esteem*, Muncie, Indiana: Accelerated Development, Inc., 1989.

Gardner, Howard. *Frames of Mind, The Theory of Multiple Intelligences*, New York: Basic Books, Inc., 1983.

Ginott, Haim. *Teacher and Child,* New York: MacMillan, 1972.

Glasser, William. *Schools Without Failure*, New York: Harper, 1966.

Gordon, Thomas. *Teacher Effectiveness Training*, New York: Peter H. Hyden, 1974.

Hartline, Jo Ellen. *Me!?,* Tucson, AZ: Zepher Press, Revised 1990

Hendricks, Gay and Wills, Russel. *The Centering Book*, Englewood Cliffs, NJ: Prentice-Hall, 1975

Hendricks, Gay and Roberts, Thomas B. *The Second Centereing Book*, Englewood Cliffs, NJ: Prentice-Hall, 1977.

Herrmann, Ned. *The Creative Brain*, Lake Lure, North Carolina: Brain Books, 1988.

Holt, John. *How Children Learn*, Revised Edition, New York: Delta/Seymour Lawrence, 1983.

Houston, Jean. *The Possible Human*, Los Angeles: J. P. Tarcher, Inc., 1982.

Jampolsky, Gerald G. *Love is Letting Go of Fear*, Millbrae, CA: Celestial Arts, 1979.

Jampolsky, Gerald G. *Teach Only Love*, New York: Bantam Books, 1983.

Jensen, Eric P. *Super Teaching*, Dubuque, Iowa: Kendall Hunt Publishing Co., 1988.

Keirsey, David and Bates, Marilyn. *Please Understand Me*, Del Mar, California: Prometheus Nemesis, 1984.

Leonard, George. *Education and Ecstacy*, New York: Dell, 1968.

Le Page, Andy, Ph.D. *Transforming Education*, Tampa, Florida: Oakmore House Press, 1987.

Resources

Maslow, Abraham. *Toward a Psychology of Being*, Princeton: Van Nostrand, 1968.

Moorman, Chick, and Dishon, Dee. *Our Classroom: We Can Learn Together*, Englewood Cliffs, NJ: Prentice Hall, 1977.

Ostrander, Sheila and Schroeder, Lynn. *Superlearning*, New York: Delacorte Press, 1979.

Palomares, U. H. and Logan, B. A. *A Curriculum on Conflict Management,* San Clemente, California: Magic Circle Publishing, 1975.

Palomares, Uvaldo, Ed.D. and Ball, Gerry, Ph.D. *Grounds for Growth*, San Clemente, California: Magic Circle Publishing, 1980.

Peck, M. Scott. *The Road Less Traveled*, New York: A Touchstone Book, Simon and Schuster, 1978.

Purkey, William. *Self-Concept and School Achievement*, Englewood Cliffs, NJ: Prentice-Hall, 1970.

Purkey, William and Novak, John. *Inviting School Success* (2nd edition). Bellmont, CA: Wadsworth Publishing Co., 1984.

Querido, René M. *Creativity in Education: the Waldorf Approach*, San Francisco, California: H. S. Dakin Co., 1982.

Reasoner, Robert. Building Self-Esteem: *Teacher's Guide and Classroom Materials* (Elementary Level), 577 College Avenue, Palo Alto, CA 94306: Consulting Psychologists Press, 1982.

Restak, Richard M., M.D. *The Mind*, New York: Bantam Books, 1988.

Rogers, Carl. *On Becoming a Person: A Therapist's View of Psychology*, Boston: Houghton Mifflin Co., 1961.

Rose, Colin. *Accelerated Learning*, New York: Dell Publishing Co., 1985.

Snitzer, Herb. *Living at Summerhill*, New York: Collier Books, 1968.

Satir, Virginia. *Self-Esteem*, Millbrae, CA: Celestial Arts, 1975.

Simon, Sidney B. *I Am Loveable and Capable*, Niles, IL: Argus, 1976.

Simon, Sidney B. *Vulture: A Modern Allegory of Putting Oneself Down*, Niles, IL: Argus, 1977.

Steiner, Claude. *The Original Warm Fuzzy Tale*, Rolling Hills Estates, CA: Jalmar Press, 1977.

Toward a State of Esteem, The Final Report of the California Task-Force to Promote Self-Esteem, and Personal and Social Responsibility, Sacramento, California: California State Department of Education, 1990.

Vitale, Barbara Meister. *Unicorns are Real: A Right-Brained Approach to Learning*, Rolling HIlls Estates, Jalmar Press, 1982.

Waitley, Denis. *The Winner's Edge*, New York: Times Books, 1980.

Waitley, Denis. *Seeds of Greatness*, Old Tappan, NJ: Felming H. Revell Company, 1983.

Weinstein, Matt and Goodman, Joel. *PLAYFAIR: Everybody's Guide to Noncompetitive Games*, New York: Doubleday/ Dolphin, 1976.

Wells, Harold C. and Canfield, Jack. *About Me (A self-concept curriculum for grades 3-6),* Chicago, IL: Encyclopedia Brittannica Educational Corporation.

The building blocks of self-esteem are skills. The more skillful a person, the more likely that he or she will be able to cope in life situations. By fostering skills of personal and social responsibility, schools can help students increase their behavioral options. Having a number of behavioral options makes it easier to make ethical choices and develop skills to function effectively.

Education and the school experience greatly influence a child's psychological and social well-being, character, and productive potential as an adult.

Toward a State of Esteem; The Final Report of the California Task Force to Promote Self-esteem and Personal and Social Responsibility, January, 1990.